Alphabet

Google is synonymous with searching, but in this innovative new research volume, Micky Lee explores how the Alphabet Corporation, now the parent company of Google, is more than just a search engine. Using a political economic approach, Lee draws on the concept of networks to investigate the growth of this key media player.

The establishment of the parent company, Alphabet, shows the company is expanding to other industries from equity investment to self-driving cars. This book first examines this history of expansion, before delving into the economic, political, and cultural profiles of the corporation. Lee ultimately finds that what makes Google powerful is not one genius idea, but rather networks of people, places, and capital.

Alphabet: The Becoming of Google is a compelling dive into the sometimes inscrutable world of Google, ideal for students, scholars, and researchers interested in the fields of digital media studies, the politics and economies of online media, and the history of the internet.

Micky Lee is an associate professor of media studies at Suffolk University, Boston, MA, USA. She has published in the areas of feminist political economy, information, technologies, and finance. Her latest books are *Understanding the Business of Global Media in the Digital Age* and *Bubbles and Machines: Gender, Information, and Financial Crises*.

Global Media Giants

Series editors: Benjamin J. Birkinbine, Rodrigo Gomez and Janet Wasko

Since the second half of the 20th century, the significance of media corporate power has been increasing in different and complex ways around the world; the power of these companies in political, symbolic, and economic terms has been a global issue and concern. In the 21st century, understanding media corporations is essential to understanding the political, economic, and socio-cultural dimensions of our contemporary societies.

The **Global Media Giants** series will continue the work that began in the series editors' book *Global Media Giants*, providing detailed examinations of the largest and most powerful media corporations in the world.

For more information about this series, please visit: https://www.routledge.com/Global-Media-Giants/book-series/GMG

Alphabet
The Becoming of Google

Micky Lee

Routledge
Taylor & Francis Group

NEW YORK AND LONDON

First published 2019
by Routledge
52 Vanderbilt Avenue, New York, NY 10017

and by Routledge
2 Park Square, Milton Park, Abingdon, Oxon, OX14 4RN

Routledge is an imprint of the Taylor & Francis Group, an informa business

© 2019 Taylor & Francis

Library of Congress Cataloging-in-Publication Data
Names: Lee, Micky, author.
Title: Alphabet: the becoming of Google/Micky Lee.
Description: First edition. | New York, NY: Routledge, 2019. |
Series: Global media giants | Includes bibliographical references and index.
Identifiers: LCCN 2019010066 (print) | LCCN 2019013987 (ebook) |
ISBN 9780429242939 (eBook) | ISBN 9780367197346 (hardback)
Subjects: LCSH: Alphabet Inc. | Google.
Classification: LCC HD9696.8.U64 (ebook) | LCC HD9696.8.U64 A44 2019
(print) | DDC 338.7/61025040973–dc23
LC record available at https://lccn.loc.gov/2019010066

ISBN: 978-0-367-19734-6 (hbk)
ISBN: 978-0-429-24293-9 (ebk)

Typeset in Times New Roman
by Deanta Global Publishing Services, Chennai, India

Contents

Illustrations

Figures

Boxes

Table

1 Introduction

"What is Google?" If Google Search is the most effective way to gather objective information to answer this question, and indeed any query, then Google Search results suggested that Google is:

1 A verb with the definition "search for information about (someone or something) on the Internet using the search engine Google".
2 A word that originates from the 1990s, the proprietary name of the search engine.
3 An American company that is most commonly known as a search engine.

Few online users would disagree with the above three definitions. However, some may be surprised that if we add "nasdaq" to the question "What is Google?", they cannot find any financial information about the company, instead they will be shown financial information about Alphabet Inc. that is traded as GOOG in the stock market. What is Alphabet? Seventeen years after Google was founded and eleven years after it became a public company, the founders Larry Page and Sergey Brin formed Alphabet, a parent company under which Google and many other companies are "collected", just like the letters A to Z are collected in the alphabet.

However, most Google users may not even be aware of the new company because Alphabet downplays the new development. The name of the parent company appears neither on Google Search's sparse, clean frontpage nor on the frontpage of YouTube, the login page of Gmail, nor Google Maps. Google is simply too well known to be called something else. If the word Google belongs to the modern lexicon and is a brand to online users, then why did the founders launch a new parent company yet keep the new company out of the spotlight? After the founding of Alphabet, is Google *being* what it used to be? Or is it *becoming* something else?

The questions about the being and becoming of Google beg other questions: What do we mean when we say: Google *is* a verb that stands for search, Google *is* a search engine, and Google *is* an American company? What if all these beings are not static, or have never been such? What if Google, the company, and Google, the search engine, have never been "things"? That their "thingness" is only assumed because they are named? If we head out to Alphabet's headquarters in Mountain View in California, move out all the furniture, disconnect all the computers, and send all the employees home for a day, will this configuration still make Alphabet a company and Google a search engine? Although the temporary evacuation is impossible, this book asks for the imagination to visualize a different configuration of a corporation.

The aims of this book are twofold: first, it offers a political economic critique of the Alphabet corporation by showing its *being* relies on capitalism and its *becoming* is also that of capitalism. In other words, the very existence of Alphabet as a corporation relies on a specific political-economic system in which change is inevitable. The business strategies, political clout, and cultural ideology of Alphabet all illustrate the limits of capitalism, in particular whether surplus capital and labor can be re-absorbed into the system. Yet, the corporation seeks to overcome the limits of capital by seeing itself as something new, something always in a becoming process. By being new and always becoming, Alphabet seeks to overcome the political-economic system that restricts its growth. To see how Alphabet accomplishes this impossible feat, I propose that an Actor-Network Theory (ANT) be applied along with a political-economic critique, because ANT enables an analysis of human–non-human interaction in value production.

The second aim of this book is to explore if computational methods of network analysis will benefit a political-economic critique of Alphabet. While political economy emphasizes capitalism as social relations, political economists usually do not quantify and visualize how these social relations look. Network analysis may also illustrate ANT's conceptualization of actors and networks because ANT rejects the existence of stable entities (such as corporations, politics). Networks are assumed to be unstable by ANT and data visualization captures a moment of being. In addition, ANT's emphasis on describing a network rather than explaining it can be illustrated by a visualization of networks.

Before I proceed further, I first disambiguate the use of Alphabet and Google in this book. I use Alphabet to refer to the technology conglomerate that serves as the parent company of Google since 2015. I use Google in two senses: first, the pre-Alphabet era from 1998 to 2015; second, the online services offered under the Google brand, most notably Google Search. The title of the book *Alphabet: The Becoming of Google* is then about the beings of two companies and how one becomes the other.

Being and Becoming

Philosophers and psychologists have written extensively about the meanings of being and becoming. The study of ontology is a study of being and reality, it seeks to understand what makes a thing a thing (Campbell, 2006). The branch of social ontology studies the nature and properties of the social world, in particular how social interaction gives rise to the existence of various entities (Epstein, 2018). The becoming of entities then relies on human beings making sense of the material world through thinking about it, naming it, and acting on it.

Becoming is also related to good and evil. Western beliefs hold that human nature is innate and humans must be changed in order to do good (Combs, 1996). For example, Judeo-Christian religions believe that humans are born sinners and they must be made good. In contrast, French philosopher Jean-Jacques Rousseau believed that humans are born good, but the outer environment can lead humans to become evil. In both beliefs, humans are born with some unchanged quality, but the quality may be changed for good (or worse) with enough guidance.

How are the above philosophical and psychological concepts of being and becoming related to a critique of Alphabet? First, Google and Alphabet are assumed to have been in a constant state of becoming. Alphabet is not just a search engine or an American company, but it is also at once an organization of employees, gender and class relations, infrastructure and buildings, culture and symbols, and so on. The state of becoming is not just about growing bigger, having more services, and gaining more customers, but it is about associating and dissociating different elements (people, buildings and infrastructure, businesses, technologies) in the network. For example, although the interface of Google Search frontpage may not have changed much since its debut, the algorithm is constantly updated. Because the algorithm is always changing, is Google Search a stable entity or has it always been a process of becoming? To give another example, the founders Larry Page and Sergey Brin have moved from being the President and CEO of Google to those of Alphabet. Google now has Sundar Pichai at the helm. Is Google the same entity despite the change in leadership? One day, if Page and Brin decided to leave Alphabet altogether, would the company be the same entity?

Second, there are no innate characteristics about a search engine and a company. The understanding of a search engine and a company has resulted from and arises with interactions between human beings and machines in a social context. What gives Google, the search engine, and Alphabet, the corporation, the properties of "things" are not only the material things (such as the buildings, the hardware inside the buildings, or the people inside the buildings), but also the languages, practices, and symbols created in social interactions between humans and machines. If the Google Search algorithm is a becoming process and if leadership can change, then what gives Alphabet the property of a "thing"? Applying Pierre Bourdieu's concept of "field theory", Hillis, Petit, and Jarrett (2013) argued that the entity of Google is a result of a field of practices. The existence of Google as a company, a search engine, and a platform is a social existence in relation to others. Relations are largely understood to be those between humans. What makes Google "real" is believed to be those social relations as well as people's awareness of the relational similarities and differences between and among practices and objects.

However, I challenge the belief that social relations can only be established between humans, because they are also established between humans and machines. The crown jewel of Alphabet, the Google Search algorithm, may appear like a "thing" because it is assumed to be a neutral tool that enables human interaction through information production and retrieval. Google Search is assumed to be a neutral tool that passively waits for humans to feed it information, and to connect humans through search. The search engine, in other words, is perceived to enable human interaction through validating relational knowledge. An example is vanity search in which users google their own names to see what information exists about them. What they seek is not so much about their own information but a validation of human relations.

However, by seeing a search engine as a process of becoming, we have to acknowledge that information does not *already* exist before the algorithm interacts with the indices. When users type in a query, they seek information as much as the algorithm seeks information from users. The search results are curated and presented by the algorithm that actively shapes how the results are interpreted. At the same time, users give feedback to the algorithm about how good the search results are. If the first few links are clicked, the algorithm will understand that the keywords are appropriately used. If no link is clicked and another search is done, then the algorithm will understand the keywords need to be refined. Using Bourdieu's concept of field of practices, human–machine interactions are often unexplored even though they play a role in shaping symbolic interactions. By seeing a machine as an active partner in social interactions, the machine learns and changes itself as much as the users do.

Network

Network is an important concept to visualize the being and becoming of Alphabet. Network has gained popular usage not only in our daily life lexicon but also in academia. Yang, Keller, and Zheng (2017) stated that networks precede digital technologies; human beings have always formed networks. But digital technologies and the rise of social media make networks become palpable in modern society. For example, online social networking sites made visual a user's online and offline connections. In academia, Castells' concept of the network society (1996) has been influential among media studies scholars because he has pointed out the paramount role that new information and communication technologies play in mediating social structure. Nevertheless, these concepts of online and offline networks all assume that humans are the agents to make connections. Technologies may be seen as tools to establish the connections but they are not seen as active agents.

In this book, the definition of network is drawn from Galloway and Thacker (2007), who defined a network as, "any system of interrelationability, biological/informatic, organic/inorganic, technical/nature. The ultimate goal is to undo the polar restrictions of the pairings" (p. 28). This definition complements with how the network is assumed in Actor-Network Theory (to be defined and explained later). ANT suggests that a network is made up of both humans and non-humans. Humans act upon non-humans, and vice versa, because both have agency. Both types of actors pick up properties of the network when they are assembled in it. Networks are always temporary because humans and non-humans are in constant assemblage and dissociation. However, a stabilized network may appear to be a *thing* where inner connections are rarely questioned. Once humans and non-humans leave the network and join others, they pick up the properties of the new network as well. To give an example related to Google Search, users' search queries probe the algorithm to process the data. In doing so, users interact with the devices on which Google is installed. A search yields an output in a recognizable way on the interface. At the user's end, the machine appears to passively respond to humans, yet the machine also has an agency because the algorithm is aware of where, when, and how the search is conducted. The accumulated information then is assumed to make the machine intelligent because it can "guess" what keywords and key phrases users will input.

In this book, I look at three implications of network. Alphabet is not just a search engine, but it is also a corporation, it relies on the Internet as a network, and it materializes a network as a "thing". The network concept has three implications in this book: first, Alphabet is a corporation in shareholder capitalism, it taps into the network of capital for resources. The network generates wealth for the shareholders. Second, the very existence of a search engine relies on the Internet, which is a network of humans and machines. Third, Google Search organizes information to materialize the network as a "thing", to give it a property of an entity. In all three implications, networks are made up of both humans and non-humans. Human actors are the users as well as Alphabet's founders, executives, board members, and employees. Non-human actors consist of technological devices (such as the computer and the mobile phone) as well as immaterial technical objects (such as protocols, algorithms, and formulae that may be immortalized in material forms such as users' manuals, contracts, and reference books). In the following, I expand the three implications of network and suggest how they will guide the inquiry in later chapters.

The first implication of seeing Alphabet as a network is that corporation is not a thing, but a nexus of contractual relationships between shareholders and executives, executives and employees, and employees and consumers. Corporations are a contractual nexus driven by signals on financial markets (Davis, 2009). Corporations do not answer to employees or consumers, but the major shareholders of corporations, namely mutual fund companies and investment banks (see Chapter 4, "Political Profile"). Stock market performance, however, directly affects employees, who are seen as disposable and can be plunged away from the network in order to trim down expenses. On the other hand, aspiring hi-tech employees are willing to take up contract jobs at Alphabet in order to increase their capital in the job market (see Chapter 5, "Cultural Profile"). I will also show that investors highly value hi-tech corporations even though they have few assets and do not have the quantity of sales in the same way as "traditional" corporations in the industries of retail and automobile (see Chapter 3, "Economic Profile"). Hi-tech companies are highly valued because they are seen as corporations that will continue to drive the economy. As a nexus in financial markets, corporations have no core or peripheral businesses. Once a branch or brand is found to hurt profit margins, those underperforming units will be dissociated from the corporation. Chapter 3, "Economic Profile", shows that Alphabet, even as a cash-rich company, halted a few services such as social media sites and Google Glass. Lastly, as a nexus, corporations carefully choose board members so that they can bring their personal and professional networks to expand the corporation's network (see Chapter 4, "Political Profile").

The second implication of seeing Alphabet as a network is that the Internet and search engine have to be understood in a historical political-economic context. Alphabet would not have existed if it had not been for the Internet. The Internet has a history, its birth relied on military money, and its earliest development relied on unpaid enthusiasts and hobbyists. Search engines also have a history that preceded the Internet (Hillis et al., 2013)—humankind had attempted to organize the world's information, as illustrated by ambitious projects such as the Egyptians building the Library of Alexandria to store all knowledge. Yet, Google Search is seen as something so new that the idea was not built on existing human wisdom. Chapter 2, "History", will show that the idea of Google Search is often portrayed as a "light bulb" moment: that the founders woke up one morning and completely figured out how an online search engine would work. The "light bulb moment" of the birth of Google Search ignores the dead labor that has contributed to the Internet infrastructure and webpages. Popular history on Google has failed to see how the founders' goal to organize the world's information capitalizes on the labor—some free, some paid—of the earliest web developers and content providers. In the popular history of Google, the company's success is often attributed to the intellect and grit of the founders, it barely mentions that Google would not have existed if not for the labor spent on the infrastructure and content. Ignoring the history of the Internet and search engines naturalizes why Google is such a dominant force in multiple facets of society. Naturalizing history makes Google a default "entry" point to the Internet on a mobile device, it eliminates alternatives by pretending that there is no history of the Internet. Ignoring the historical context of the Internet and search engines also makes Alphabet appear to be a company that is starkly different from companies in "old" industries such as retail, energy, and the automobile industry. Because Alphabet is in the business of "newness", the organization is believed to have none of the woes that plague other organizations, such as sluggish sales, workplace inequity, or sexual harassment (see Chapter 5, "Cultural Profile").

The third implication of seeing Alphabet as a network is that human–human and human–non-human relations can be visualized by applying computational methods of network analysis. As Alphabet is in a constant state of becoming, it is never a stable entity with fixed relations. Network analysis is therefore effective at showing what constitutes Google's economy, politics, and culture. The third implication will be delineated more after a discussion of the theoretical frameworks of the political economy of communication and Actor-Network Theory (ANT).

Theoretical Frameworks

The critique in this book is grounded in the branch of political economy of communication advanced by Janet Wasko, Eileen Meehan, Vincent Mosco, Herb Schiller, and Dan Schiller. Although these scholars focus on different industries and examine specific aspects of digital capitalism, they are all concerned that the power of corporations overwhelms all forms of political and social life, leaving little room for the commons to thrive. The Global Media Giants series, to which this book belongs, seeks to examine how a number of media corporations consolidate power across political, economic, and cultural realms.

It is worthwhile reviewing why the series editors think it is imperative to study media and hi-tech corporations. Birkinbine, Gómez, and Wasko (2017) wrote that technology companies have moved from selling packaged software to collecting users' data to commodify them for advertisers. Furthermore, "technological convergence, digital (economic) disruption, and increased interconnectivity have been heralded as harbingers of an entirely new epoch to human history" (p. 2). But these "new" developments have done little to stabilize the global economy or eliminate financial crisis. The rise of global corporations parallels the growing wealth gap between the wealthiest populations and the poorest. Not only is the widening wealth gap unjust, but it also erodes the roles that government and community play in political, economic, and social lives. Media owned by conglomerates are reluctant to critique economic injustice, rendering alternative worldviews and ways of life invisible. To afford an alternative worldview, "a comparative analysis and ongoing reassessment of the world's largest and most powerful media corporations' changing structures and practices is vitally important" (p. 3).

Alphabet, being a powerful technology company, serves as a case study to show how a company may appear to overcome the limits of capitalism by stabilizing the global economy, yet it reinforces unequal power relations between owners and users, and the best-paid engineers and contract workers. In the following, I first discuss what books on Google are available in the market, then the literature that critiques the company and the search engine.

Books about Google

The popular book market is not short of titles about Google, most of them are technical and business books. The WorldCat library catalog shows that between 1998 (the year when Google was founded) and 2018, 5,226 printed books have "Google" in the title. Technical books and business books rarely critique Google because the former teach readers how to optimize Google applications and services (such as Google Analytics, Google AdWords, and Google Maps), the latter educate readers in the secrets of Google's success, hoping the inspired readers will launch an equally successful business. Some early titles of trade books include: *The Search: How Google and its Rivals Rewrote the Roles of Business and Transformed Our Culture* (Battelle, 2005), *The Google Story* (Vise & Malseed, 2006), *Google Speaks: Secrets of the World's Greatest Billionaire Entrepreneurs, Sergey Brin and Larry Page* (Lowe, 2009), *Googled: The End of the World as We Know It* (Auletta, 2009). Quality among these trade books varies, but they tend to follow the "Great Men Histories" storyline, as I will lay out in Chapter 2, "History". In this narrative, the story begins with the childhood and education of the two founders, their ideas about organizing the world's information, and the challenges they faced about funding. The story continues to recount how Google grew bigger and eventually went public. Most trade books celebrate the company instead of offering an objective evaluation of the trials and tribulations of the company. They also fail to mention the political-economic system in which Google was founded. The omission is not surprising given most business books pitch to readers who want to become successful capitalistic entrepreneurs.

While most trade books rely on secondary sources, some have primary sources that intend to provide "insider's information"; some of these titles are *Googled* (Auletta, 2009), *In the Plex: How Google Thinks, Works, and Shapes Our Lives* (Levy, 2011), and *Google: How Google Works* (Schmidt & Rosenberg, 2014). Auletta (2009) and Levy (2011) managed to interview a large number of key players inside Google, giving a more complex view of the decision-making process within the company. Schmidt and Rosenberg (2014), being former major Google executives, give anecdotes of how Google's management style, corporate strategy, and work culture differ from other companies.

Recent trade books also show that Google has a number of rivals in Silicon Valley. For example, Gilder (2018) situated Google in the hi-tech industry where commercialization has taken over innovation and personal privacy is at stake. Some books compare the competition between Google and other hi-tech companies, showing well-plotted tactics and expensive lawsuits that undermine each other. Two titles are: *Dogfight: How Apple and Google Went to War and Started a Revolution* (Vogelstein, 2013) and *Digital Wars: Apple, Google, Microsoft and the Battle for the Internet* (Arthur, 2014).

In academia, scholars who subscribe to a critical perspective have offered their thoughts on Google—the company and the search engine. Here I first summarize major work on Google from a political-economic perspective, then I examine some academic books that critique Google. Due to space constraints, I have excluded books that focus on Google as well as other hi-tech companies.

Political economists have asked questions such as: How do political, economic, and cultural power structures enable Google's growth and the eventual domination of the search market? How does Google commodify information and how does this process inform capitalism? In my first book on Google, *Free Information: The Case Against Google* (Lee, 2010), I applied a political economic approach informed by Mosco (2004) and Schiller (2007) to debunk the notion of "free information". I questioned how users share personal information with Google in exchange for free services, how Google negotiated with the Chinese government to provide dissidents' personal information, how Google acquired geospatial mapping technology that was developed with public money, as well as how Google Books obscured the labor that went into book scanning.

How Google commodifies personal information is a main thrust of political economic work. For example, Kang and McAllister (2011) suggested that Google commodifies the audience and its consciousness while the audience provides free labor for Google. Pasquinelli (2009) suggested that the political economy of Google is that of the search algorithm: value accumulation comes from the economies of attention (which depends on the attention capital of the whole network) and of cognition (which in turn made it possible for Google to be a "rentier" of the Internet). To Caraway (2011), "the media owner rents the use of the medium to the industrial capitalist who is interested in gaining access to an audience" (p. 701).

Fuchs (2011, 2012) and Fuchs and Winseck (2011) made a significant contribution to the understanding of Google's capital accumulation process. Fuchs modified Marx's M-C-M' (money-commodity-more money) model to show that Google's capital accumulation model can be represented by M-C $\ldots$ P_1 – P_2 $\ldots$ C' – M'. The process begins with Google investing money (M) to buy capital (C), in the forms of labor power and technology. Google employees provide services (P_1) for users, which services cannot be counted as commodities because most are provided free of charge. The popularity of Google's free services leads to a large number of users performing unpaid labor (P_2) both by generating data through searches and by producing web content. Google users (C') are then the double objects of commodification because "(1) they and their data are Internet prosumer commodities themselves; (2) through this commodification their consciousness becomes, while online, permanently exposed to commodity logic in the form of advertisements" (Fuchs, 2011, para. 21). Finally, M' is the money that Google makes from advertising.

Spreeuwenberg and Poell (2012) and Paŝko (2018) respectively examined the political economy of algorithms and operating platforms. Paŝko (2018) suggested that algorithms are artifacts that dominate and control society under a rationality that favors commodity exchange and high profit rates. Google algorithms are argued to rationalize management styles, audience commodity, and surplus value. Spreeuwenberg and Poell (2012) stated that Alphabet gave Android operating systems, at no cost, to hardware manufacturers in exchange for more users using Google apps. Alphabet controls the development of Android and dictates to manufacturers that they design hardware that is compatible with the operating system.

Scholars and public intellectuals have written a number of books to critique Google, in particular how it exercises power to influence an understanding of information, knowledge, self, and society. Some of the titles are: *Google and the Myth of Universal Knowledge: A View from Europe* (Jeanneney, 2007) *Search Engine Society* (Halavais, 2009), *Deep Search: The Politics of Search Beyond Google* (Becker & Stalder, 2009), *The Googlization of Everything* (Vaidhyanathan 2011), *Google and the Digital Divide: The Bias of Online Knowledge* (Segev, 2010), *Google and the Culture of Search* (Hillis et al., 2013), *When Google Met Wikileaks* (Assange, 2014), and *Algorithms of Oppression: How Search Engines Reinforce Racism* (Noble, 2018). While some books have a specific concern, such as US-centric knowledge (Jeanneney, 2007; Segev, 2010) or anti-blackness (Noble, 2018), a few themes were found in the critiques. First, the search algorithm is critiqued to be less than objective because its algorithm prioritizes sites that are already popular (Halavais, 2009; Lobet-Maris, 2009; Vaidhyanathan, 2011). The search results are critiqued to provide good over best answers to queries (Halavais, 2009). Services such as Google News personalizes services that effectively "fracture … a sense of common knowledge or common priorities" (Vaidhyanathan, 2011, p. 139). The search engine also reinforces inequalities in information access because it gravitates toward commercial and popular sites (Segev, 2010) as well as sites written in English (Jeanneney, 2007; Segev, 2010).

Second, information privacy is a big concern among scholars and public intellectuals: Google compromises users' privacy by showing their faces and houses in Google Maps (Vaidhyanathan, 2011), by using unexpired cookies, and by making individual data searchable (Halavais, 2009). It is unknown what will happen to the data when Google ceases to exist—given that companies rarely last for more than a century (Halavais, 2009).

Third, Google is said to believe that it is a benevolent, humanitarian force even though it is a profit-making business (Assange, 2014; Vaidhyanathan, 2011). The reliance on a private company to provide a seemingly free service diminishes support for public investment and the common good (Hillis et al., 2013). Assange (2014) suggested that Jigsaw (formerly Google Ideas), the think-tank of Google, took up the responsibility of foreign affairs offices, attempting to intervene in international relations on behalf of the US government. It effectively sees itself as a government agency than as a company unit. Google's friendliness with the US government also means that it has no problem with sharing sensitive satellite images with the US military.

Lastly, Google has changed online culture to a great extent. The term "googlization" was coined by Vaidhyanathan (2011) to show how Google has permeated culture and affected how users view themselves, the world, and human knowledge. Hillis et al. (2013) added that Google has achieved a sacred status in society by instilling a culture of search. This culture plays a central role to acquire knowledge and produce meanings while changing the relationship between individuals and society. Showing how African Americans are symbolically oppressed by a search engine, Noble (2018) argues that digital decision reinforces oppressive social relationships and enacts new modes of racial profiling. For example, imaging software identifies African Americans as apes while sexually objectifying black women.

Current books have offered critiques of the company and search engine from different perspectives. However, most books still seem to see Google as a search engine company than a technology conglomerate that expands its reach beyond online search. Not viewing it as a technology conglomerate understates the power that Alphabet has over political, economic, and social lives.

Why Another Book on Google?

The markets of trade and academic books have no shortage of titles on Google, so why is this volume needed? What this volume adds to existing studies is that it highlights how the *becoming* of a technology company is a process of capital attempting to overcome the limits of capitalism. While critical scholars have pointed out that digital divide, racism, and privacy violation are related to the profit-seeking nature of Google, they have not explicated how these problems may be political economic as well as social and cultural. In other words, digital divide and racism can be seen as what David Harvey (2011) called spatiotemporal differences: the flow of capital creates temporal and spatial differentiation, yet it feeds on this differentiation to thrive. What it means is that the uneven technological development of mobile telephony and broadband Internet can be understood as a result of concentrated wealth in specific countries and communities, yet these gaps legitimize capital to expand to different spaces in the name of bridging spatial differences and helping some populations to catch up in the digital age.

While adopting a political economy of communication as a theoretical framework, I am mindful to not let previous political economic critique limit my imagination of the relation between information and capital. I do not accept that Alphabet, the corporation, is a stable entity. Similarly, I refuse to see Alphabet's main product "information" as a monolithic "thing" that has the same property across platforms. ANT advocates that information bears the property of the technologies that produce and distribute it. ANT also assumes that humans are not the only agency in networks, non-humans (animals, plants, machines, buildings, infrastructure) also have agency. Lastly, political economic critique can benefit from computational methods such as network analysis that illustrates relations between actors. Such methods also show the relations between humans and non-humans, illustrating how power and capital are generated in networks.

The first gap in the current political-economic critique of information is that information is treated as a monolithic commodity. Political economists see information as a common good that becomes a commodity when it is assigned with an exchange value in the market (Schiller, 2007). Others see that the production of information puts an unnecessary strain on surplus value in productive activities (McChesney, Wood, & Foster, 1998). For example, money spent on the advertising and marketing of a commodity takes away the "real" value produced by the workers who make the commodity. I have argued that digital information is not monolithic and homogeneous (Lee, 2014), it alters the material conditions in which it is produced, distributed, and consumed while exerting symbolic power on producers and users (Lee, 2019). An example to show that information is not homogeneous is

Google Maps information: mapping information is understood differently when it is used on a desktop and a mobile phone. When Google Maps is used on a desktop, the users *look* at or *read* the information. When Google Maps is used on the mobile map, the users may *hear* the information. An example of information exerting symbolic power on users is that the algorithm of search engines changes because of users' input. The algorithm learns what words are commonly spelled incorrectly by users. When enough users input an incorrect spelling, the algorithm autocorrects the typo and uses the correct spelling instead. Over time, the users believe that Google can guess what they think not only because it corrects spelling errors, but also because it offers suggestions for keywords. The assumed superb prediction power gives Google Search a symbolic power over users.

The second gap in a political-economic critique of a corporation is that it indicates that only humans have agency. This book recognizes that both human and non-human actors have agency in a network. The aforementioned example of algorithm changes to respond to human actions shows that a non-human actor has a sense of agency. ANT scholars believe that the sense of agency is given in a network (Callon, 1998) because actors are network effects, they take up the network's attributes (Law, 1999). The most controversial ANT assumption is that there is no macrostructure—such as society, politics, and economy—there are only actors and networks. In the words of one of the most well-known ANT scholars, Bruno Latour (1999), we should examine "interactions through various kinds of devices, inscriptions, forms, and formulae, into a very local, very practical, and tiny locus" (p. 17). Because context flows through networks, agency is not separated from structure. ANT's insistence on the inseparable agency from structure may go against a common sociological view that human actions reinforce or challenge structure. For example, when Alphabet employees carried out a massive walkout in November 2018, political economists suggested that workers exercised their agency to challenge an unfair socioeconomic structure fostered by Alphabet. ANT scholars however would see those workers dissociate from their usual networks (such as work computers or other co-workers) and associate themselves with new networks (such as the streets or workers who belong to different units and companies). The streets, as a non-human actor, then are attributed with a meaning; they are no longer avenues that take employees to work, but they provide visibility to the demonstrating workers.

The third gap that this book fills in is some experimentation regarding whether political economists could benefit from empirical data generated by computational methods network analysis. Because Alphabet is a network consisting of both humans and non-humans, computational methods will be useful to visualize who the actors are and how they relate to each other. Political economic work in the field of communication does not subscribe to one or two specific

research methods but document analysis is commonly used. Political economists, however, are wary of quantitative methods such as survey and experiment
largely because they are grounded in the post-positivist tradition that critical
scholars found to be reductionist. However, political economists believe in a
realist epistemology (Mosco, 2009), which means reality is mutually constituted by discourse and social practice. To this end, empirical data generated by a
computational method of network analysis should benefit a political-economic
analysis because networks capture a moment of a constituted reality: how the
reality is talked about, and how it is enacted by social practices.

I expect skepticism about the compatibility of a political economy of communication and ANT (see discussion in Lee, 2014; Lee, 2019) due to their
fundamental disagreement about whether social structures exist or not. I also
expect skepticism about whether computational methods are simply complex
but unnecessary methods for illustrating data for a political-economic critique. While I do not think this volume will quench such doubts, these questions will hopefully generate discussion among media studies scholars. In the
concluding chapter, I will discuss how the case study of Alphabet illustrates
the compatibility of political economy and ANT as well as the usefulness of
computational methods.

A Note on Texts and Methods

The analysis relies on data drawn from a range of documents retrieved from
Google Search. Sometimes I knew what documents I was searching for and
the search engine returned with the anticipated results. For example, I needed
information about Alphabet's annual filings with the US Securities and
Exchange Commission so I typed in "Alphabet 10K" and the first result led
me to the report on Alphabet's site for investors. In another instance, I needed
information about institutional holdings of Alphabet's stocks so I typed in
"who owned Alphabet nasdaq" and the second link led me to the nasdaq.com
site on stock details. Because both 10K reports and stock information are for
investors and analysts, the information has already been externally verified.

At other times, I used Google Search to understand how the algorithm and
content providers constitute the worldview of search results. I was not looking
for a particular document, but a group of documents that were mathemati-
cally calculated to be the most relevant to my queries according to Google.
For example, in Chapter 2, "History", I wanted to know which sites would
be deemed most relevant to "Google history". I did not see those sites being
the most authoritative, accurate, or even relevant, but the search results gave
insights into both what the Google Search algorithm "thinks" is the most relevant and how website owners "game" the system to land top spots. I analyzed
these results using a number of methods: narrative analysis (see Chapter 2,

"History"), discourse analysis (see Chapter 5, "Cultural Profile"), and text mining and network analysis (see Chapter 2, "History", and Chapter 4, "Political Profile"). Since computational methods are less frequently used in political economic critiques, I state and explain some terminology in the following.

Computational methods in social science refer to those that require the computer to generate and analyze a large dataset that provides insights into society. Applying such methods requires collaboration between social scientists, computer scientists, and statisticians. Data that are drawn from the Internet, sensor networks, and crowdsourcing systems will be processed by software in machine learning, statistics, social network analysis, and natural language processing (Mason, Vaughan, & Wallach, 2013).

In Chapter 2, "History", I used text mining to generate keywords used for network analysis. In particular, I used the software Octoparse and Outwit to do "web scraping". Web scraping refers to the process of extracting keywords or texts from a collection of webpages (Ignatow & Mihalcea, 2017). After gathering the keywords from webpages, I used the network analysis to deduce the relationships between the keywords and the webpages. Network analysis was also used in Chapter 4, "Political Profile", when I sought to understand the relations between shareholders of hi-tech companies, lobbyists, and lobbying of issues, as well as key decision-makers, in Alphabet.

A network consists of nodes and relations between them. Nodes are connected by relations of various types (Yang et al., 2017). They are the units of observations and can be persons, places, organizations, objects, and so on. The network graphs are descriptive, showing the relations between nodes. Sometimes the relations are binary (they either exist or they do not) and sometimes they have a value (to what degree the relations exist between nodes). I used the data visualization software Gephi to produce the graphs. More explanations will be provided in the relevant chapters about what meanings may be interpreted from the graphs.

Chapter Outline

The editors of the Global Media Giants series to which this book belongs prescribed a specific chapter structure because they recognized that the multifaceted power of corporations needs to be understood economically, politically, and culturally. Individual authors were, however, encouraged to modify the chapter structure when they saw fit. In Chapter 2, "History", I have not attempted to provide an "objective" account of Alphabet history because, when compared to the history of some older media companies, Alphabet is a relatively young company. In addition, the history of Alphabet is the history of the Internet, and information about the company's history is more readily available on the Internet than in books. Therefore, I aim to find out what Google history is according to Google Search. After gathering the top ten websites about Google history as well as the biographies of the two founders, I use both narrative analysis and network analysis to examine the significant events, technological developments, and key players highlighted by these most "relevant" webpages. The narrative of Google history shows that the first stage—from the births of the two founders to Google becoming a public company—has a clear storyline: who, when, where, and what events moved the story along. The narrative of the second stage, the expansion of Google thereafter, and the third stage, the founding of Alphabet, is relatively unfocused. Webpages offered little explanation of why Google had to keep expanding or why it founded a parent company. The narrative lacks a historical political-economic context, meaning the history of Alphabet was not related to broader sociopolitical changes. Network analysis of keywords drawn from the webpages of Google history also informs that the history of Alphabet is devoid of a historical political-economic context: the most popular keywords are search applications as well as competitors (such as Microsoft and Yahoo!).

In Chapter 3, "Economic Profile", I address the issues of financial data and market share; corporate structure and properties; typical strategies; and new developments. The concept of capital as a network is used to guide the discussion of how Alphabet needs to constantly encourage more and more of the world's population to go online and to encourage more online users to use Google services plus the Android operating system. I first argue that Alphabet is a continuation of Google rather than a new development because the majority of revenue still comes from advertising. Because online advertising is not just about selling time or space, but also unique searches performed by users, Google Search needs to ensure that there are more searches on the Google platform.

In Chapter 4, "Political Profile", I address the issues of ownership; ties to the state and lobbying efforts; board of directors and interlocks. The editors asked the authors to address labor and social marketing in this chapter but I choose to address labor in Chapter 5, "Cultural Profile", due to space constraints. In this chapter, I examine power as a network. I argue that networks produce and distribute power to individuals and organizations who are not powerful on their own. I first look at the institutional owners of Alphabet as well as other hi-tech companies such as Microsoft and Amazon. I show that these hi-tech companies are owned by mutual fund companies and investment banks that also own each other! Next I examine the relations between Alphabet's board of directors and their associated organizations. I find that a few universities, professional associations, and capital venture firms have enormous power in Alphabet's corporate governance. Lastly, I look at the lobbying efforts of Alphabet to find out which political issues concern the company the most. Other organizations that share the same concerns tend to be corporations and trade groups more than labor unions.

In Chapter 5, "Cultural Profile", the editors asked the authors to address symbolic universe and ideology; popular products/services and everyday life; as well as cultural exports/imports to/from other countries. I take the liberty of interpreting culture as the work culture of Alphabet. The Internet as a historical, materialist network is used to critique online culture that is assumed to be culturally neutral. The assumption of the Internet lacking a history reinforces the ideology that Alphabet and other hi-tech companies provide a new kind of organizational structure. However, the massive walkouts of Alphabet workers around the globe show that the labor issues that trouble the "old" organizations are alive and well in Alphabet. Some of these issues include the income disparity between full-time workers and temporary workers and the racialized and gendered managerial structures. Because I believe that it is urgent to address labor practices in an organization that prides itself on meritocracy, I decided not to address popular products/services and cultural exports/imports to/from other countries. These issues are mentioned but not discussed in Chapter 3, "Economic Profile".

In Chapter 6, "Conclusion", I assess the usefulness of the network concept in understanding Alphabet. I find the political-economic assumption of a macrostructure to be contradictory of the network concept because actors do not necessarily isolate economic motivations from political and cultural ones. The book series' separation of the economic from the political and cultural realms seems to limit the fluidity of the network concept. Despite this, drawing on ANT and computational methods of network analysis to understand Alphabet fills three current gaps in a political-economic critique of information: it calls attention to the property of information; it takes into account the agency of non-human actors; and it provides empirical data for a visualization of power that is produced and circulated in networks. However, document analysis alone is insufficient to fully realize the potential of ANT, interviews and ethnographic studies are also required to understand how humans interact with machines and the material world.

Bibliography

Arthur, C. (2014). *Digital wars: Apple, Google, Microsoft and the battle for the Internet* (2nd ed.). London: Kogan Page.

Assange, J. (2014). *When Google met Wikileaks*. New York: OR Books.

Auletta, K. (2009). *Googled: The end of the world as we know it*. New York: Penguin.

Battelle, J. (2005). *The search: How Google and its rivals rewrote the rules of businesses and transformed our culture*. New York: Portfolio.

Becker, K., & Stalder, F. (Eds.). (2009). *Deep search: The politics of search beyond Google*. Innsbruck, Austria: StudienVerlag.

Birkinbine, B. J., Gómez, R., & Wasko, J. (2017). Introduction. In: B. J. Birkinbine, R. Gomez, & J. Wasko (Eds.), *Global media giants* (pp. 1–7). New York: Routledge.

Callon, M. (1998). An essay on framing and overflowing: Economic externalities revisited by sociology. In: M. Callon (Ed.), *The laws of the market* (pp. 244–269). Oxford, UK: Blackwell.

Campbell, K. (2006). Ontology. In: D. M. Borchert (Ed.), *Encyclopedia of philosophy* (2nd ed.) (Vol. 7, pp. 21–27). Detroit, MI: Macmillan Reference.

Caraway, B. (2011). Audience labor in the new media environment: A Marxian revisiting of the audience commodity. *Media, Culture and Society*, *33*(5), 693–708.

Castells, M. (1996). *The rise of the network society*. Cambridge, MA: Blackwell Publishing.

Combs, A. (1996). *Being and becoming: A field approach to psychology*. New York: Springer.

Davis, G. F. (2009). *Managed by markets: How finance re-shaped America*. Oxford, UK: Oxford University Press.

Epstein, B. (2018). Social ontology. In: E. N. Zalta (Ed.), *The Stanford encyclopedia of philosophy*. Retrieved from: https://plato.stanford.edu/archives/sum2018/entries/social-ontology/. Accessed: 4th April, 2019.

Fuchs, C. (2011). A contribution to the critique of the political economy of Google. *Fast Capitalism*, *8*(1). Retrieved from: www.fastcapitalism.com/. Accessed: 4th April, 2019.

Fuchs, C. (2012). Google capitalism. *Triple C: Cognition, Communication, Co-operation*, *10*(1), 42–48.

Fuchs, C., & Winseck, D. (2011). Critical media and communication studies today: A conversation. *Triple C: Cognition, Communication, Co-operation*, *9*(2), 247–271.

Galloway, A. R., & Thacker, E. (2007). *Exploit: A theory of network*. Minneapolis, MN: University of Minnesota Press.

Gilder, G. (2018). *Life after Google: The fall of Big Data and the rise of blockchain economy*. Washington, DC: Regnery Gateway.

Halavais, A. (2009). *Search engine society*. Cambridge, UK: Polity.

Harvey, D. (2011). *The enigma of capital*. New York: Oxford University Press.

Hillis, K., Petit, M., & Jarrett, K. (Eds.). (2013). *Google and the culture of search*. New York: Routledge.

Ignatow, G., & Mihalcea, R. (2017). *Text mining: A guidebook for the social sciences*. Thousand Oaks, CA: Sage.

Jeanneney, J. N. (2007). *Google and the myth of universal knowledge: A view from Europe*. Chicago, IL: University of Chicago Press.

Kang, H., & McAllister, M. (2011). Selling you and your clicks: Examining the audience commodification of Google. *Triple C: Cognition, Communication, Co-operation*, *9*(2), 141–153.

Latour, B. (1999). On recalling ANT. In: J. Law & J. Hassard (Eds.), *Actor network theory and after* (pp. 15–25). Oxford, UK: Blackwell.

Law, J. (1999). After ANT: Complexity, naming and topology. In: J. Law & J. Hassard (Eds.), *Actor network theory and after* (pp. 1–14). Oxford, UK: Blackwell.

Lee, M. (2010). *Free information? The case against Google*. Champaign, IL: Common Ground.

Lee, M. (2014). What can political economists learn from economic sociologists? A case study of NASDAQ. *Communication, Culture, and Critique*, *7*(2), 246–263.

Lee, M. (2019). *Bubbles and machines: Gender, information, and financial crises.* London: University of Westminster Press.

Levy, S. (2011). *In the plex: How Google thinks, works, and shapes our lives.* New York: Simon & Schuster.

Lobet-Maris, C. (2009). From trust to tracks: A technology assessment perspective revisited. In: K. Becker & F. Stalder (Eds.), *Deep search: The politics of search beyond Google* (pp. 73–84). Innsbruck, Austria: StudienVerlag.

Lowe, J. (2009). *Google speaks: Secrets of the world's greatest billionaire entrepreneurs, Sergey Brin and Larry Page.* Hoboken, NJ: John Wiley and Sons.

Mason, W., Vaughan, J. W., & Wallach, H. (2013). Computational social science and social computing. *Machine Learning, 95*(3), 257–260.

McChesney, R. W., Wood, E. M., & Foster, J. B. (1998). *Capitalism and the information age: The political economy of the global communication revolution.* New York: Monthly Review Press.

Mosco, V. (2004). *The digital sublime: Myth, power, and cyberspace.* Cambridge, MA: MIT Press.

Noble, S. U. (2018). *Algorithm of oppression: How search engines reinforce racism.* New York: NYU Press.

Paŝko, B. (2018). A critique of the political economy of algorithms: A brief history of Google's technological rationality. *Triple C: Cognition, Communication, Co-operation, 16*(1), 315–331.

Pasquinelli, M. (2009). Google's PageRank: Diagram of the cognitive capitalism and rentier of the common intellect. In: K. Becker & F. Stalder (Eds.), *Deep search: The politics of search beyond Google* (pp. 152–162). Innsbruck, Austria: StudienVerlag.

Schiller, D. (2007). *Digital capitalism: Networking and global market system.* Cambridge, MA: MIT Press.

Schmidt, E., & Rosenberg, J. (2014). *Google: How Google works.* New York: Grand Central Publishing.

Segev, E. (2010). *Google and the digital divide: The bias of online knowledge.* Oxford, UK: Chandes.

Spreeuwenberg, K., & Poell, T. (2012). Android and the political economy of the mobile Internet: A renewal of open source critique. *First Monday, 17*(7). Retrieved from: https://journals.uic.edu/ojs/index.php/fm/article/view/4050/3271. Accessed: 4th April, 2019.

Vaidhyanathan, S. (2011). *The Googlization of everything (And why we should worry).* Berkeley, CA: University of California Press.

Vise, D. A., & Malseed, M. (2006). *The Google story.* New York: Delta.

Vogelstein, F. (2013). *Dogfight: How Apple and Google went to war and started a revolution.* New York: Sarah Crichton Books.

Yang, S., Keller, F. B., & Zheng, L. (2017). *Social network analysis: Methods and examples.* Thousand Oaks, CA: Sage.

2 History

What Google Search Tells Us About the History of Google

Google Search claims to organize online information and provide relevant results to any queries. If this is the case, then what is the history of Google according to Google Search? In this chapter, I want to know how the search algorithm constructs the ontology of Google history. I also want to know how content providers "game" the algorithm so that their pages about Google history will secure top spots on search results. The history that is intersubjectively shaped by humans and machines will then be analyzed by the methods of narrative analysis and social network analysis. Both methods will reveal the ontology of Google history: who play key roles, what were the major events, and how Google became successful.

The ontology of search results about Google's history needs to be critiqued because Google Search evaluates and organizes online information in a specific way. However, the pervasive use of Google Search means that this worldview has been accepted as the easiest and fastest—if not the best and the only—way to find out information. According to Internet Live Stats, Google Search processes 40,000 searches per second or 1.2 trillion searches a year. On average, everyone in the world conducts 158 searches on Google in a year. Moreover, 78% of online searches around the world are done on Google.

Critics believe that search engines do not present neutral information: how a search engine selects, organizes, and presents information can destroy or invisibly distort the context (Jeanneney, 2007). Google Search, in particular, was said to value popularity over accuracy, established sites over new ones (Vaidhyanathan, 2011), and to act as a gatekeeper that indexes, organizes, and customizes information (Segev, 2010).

What does Google say about its worldview of information organization? According to "How Search works",[1] the first step of the machine is to crawl all existing webpages and organize information in the Search index. The crawlers then find links on these webpages and go a few levels deeper to crawl the linked sites. The crawling process is an intersubjective human–machine effort: although Google says "computer programs" decide which sites to crawl, webmasters of pages can also ask Google to crawl their pages. Next Google says "systems" will render the content of the page and keep track of it in the Search index. At the users' end, when a query is made, search algorithms will consult the index. Google sees search algorithms as an active partner during the search: they detect incorrect spellings, guess what the search is once the user has typed in a few letters, suggest keywords, and determine if the expected answer is narrow or broad. Next, algorithms rank webpages based on relevance determined by "hundred[s] of different factors": new information, rank of websites, and the number of links on the websites. Lastly, algorithms are said to have the ability to tailor answers by taking into account a user's country and location.

While critics are definite that Google Search is a gatekeeper and Google claims that the algorithms are intelligent, it may be worthwhile finding out how Google Search answers the query of Google history. The purpose is not to decide how accurate or objective the answers are, or to evaluate if the answers are the best or the most relevant. The purpose is to find out how knowledge is intersubjectively constructed both by the algorithms and by the content providers: content providers produce content to be crawled by the algorithms; algorithms rank the websites; content providers change information on the websites in response to the algorithms. In order to find out such knowledge, I used methods of narrative analysis and social network analysis. Narrative analysis is useful at understanding the stories that people tell in a culture and the learned values (Akinsanya & Bach, 2014). Narrative is more than a series of events, but also how the stories acquire meanings in a culture (Jovchelovitch & Bauer, 2000). If the same story is told in the same way across narratives and if the lessons learned are similar, then the story can be called an ideology, a set of beliefs shared in a culture that seeks to explain why things are a certain way. Social network analysis is useful at showing the bridge between micro and macro levels (Yang, Keller, & Zheng, 2017). Here, the micro level is keywords on individual webpages and the macro level is the story of Google as reflected from the frequent key persons, organizations, and events on the webpages. I will suggest how the results of social network analysis reinforce those of narrative analysis and will conclude the chapter by discussing how social network analysis may enrich a political economic critique.

Narrative Analysis

Narrative analysis examines how a story "decipher[s] and transfer[s] information" (Akinsanya & Bach, 2014, p. 1). Narrative tells a company's history by including a beginning, a series of events, and perhaps, sometimes, the end. It also states who the main actors are, what actions they take, and what consequences those actions had. Narrative may also explain actors' motivations and evaluate their deeds. By looking at a number of narratives about Alphabet's history, I deduced the patterns and anomalies of the stories. If there is a noticeable pattern, then there is a consensus of what values are shared in an online culture dominated by the English language. These values teach social beings how to behave, what to aspire for, and how to explain cultural phenomena.

I gathered from Google Search the top ten links of each of three searches generated by the queries: Larry Page biography, Sergey Brin biography, and history of Google (all without quotation marks). The search results are in Box 2.1. Next, I printed out the webpages, skimmed through the content and deduced ten topics about the history of Google (listed in Box 2.2). Because the history of Google is presented as a chronological order of events, so the topics are grouped into three phases: (1) from the founders' births to the moment when Google became a publicly-traded company; (2) Google as a public company; and (3) the restructuring of Google into Alphabet. In the following, I summarize what each of the topics entails in the history of Google.

Box 2.1: Top Ten Links of Three Searches Conducted on Google Search on 5th December, 2017

Sergey Brin Biography

www.biography.com/people/sergey-brin-12103333
www.thefamouspeople.com/profiles/sergey-brin-3349.php
https://en.wikipedia.org/wiki/Sergey_Brin
https://astrumpeople.com/sergey-brin-biography/
www.businessinsider.com/the-successful-life-of-google-cofounder-sergey
    -brin-2015-8
www.notablebiographies.com/news/Ow-Sh/Page-Larry-and-Brin-Sergey.html
www.britannica.com/biography/Sergey-Brin
www.famousinventors.org/sergey-brin
www.bloomberg.com/research/stocks/people/person.asp?personId=5346
    04&privcapId=29096
www.forbes.com/profile/sergey-brin/

Larry Page Biography

www.biography.com/people/larry-page-12103347
https://en.wikipedia.org/wiki/Larry_Page
www.businessinsider.com/the-life-career-of-larry-page-2016-3
www.thefamouspeople.com/profiles/larry-page-3344.php
www.forbes.com/profile/larry-page/
www.notablebiographies.com/news/Ow-Sh/Page-Larry-and-Brin-Sergey.html

www.britannica.com/biography/Larry-Page
www.itpro.co.uk/strategy/leadership/22753/larry-page-biography-salary-
    and-career-history-of-google-s-co-founder-and
www.famous-entrepreneurs.com/larry-page
www.youtube.com/watch?v=P7TEqoEWtrc

History of Google

www.google.com/intl/en/about/our-story/
https://en.wikipedia.org/wiki/Google
https://en.wikipedia.org/wiki/History_of_Google
www.wired.com/2005/08/battelle/
www.youtube.com/watch?v=Quk88piD8PM
https://myactivity.google.com/myactivity
www.internethistorypodcast.com/2017/04/the-history-of-google/
www.thoughtco.com/who-invented-google-1991852
https://interestingengineering.com/almost-everything-you-need-to-know-
    about-googles-history
www.britannica.com/topic/Google-Inc

Box 2.2: Topics in the History of Google

Phase 1: Before Google Initial Public Offering (IPO)

1 Background: founders' birthplaces, childhood, family, and education
2 Partnership and mentorship
3 First invention: what it is, how it works, and why it is important
4 Fund-raising and initial public offering (IPO)

Phase 2: Google as a Public Company

5 Acquisitions
6 Innovation and global expansion
7 Philanthropy
8 Controversies
9 Google campus and infrastructure

Phase 3: Alphabet

10 Restructuring

Phase 1: Before Google Initial Public Offering (IPO)

The four topics in the first phase are: (1) Background: founders' birthplaces, childhood, family, and education; (2) partnership and mentorship; (3) first invention: what it is, how it works, and why it is important; and (4) fund-raising and initial public offering (IPO). Childhood experience and educational background are implied to make men *become* great. Nevertheless, the potential of great men has to be encouraged by others—namely, other great men of a similar or higher position. Catalysis is believed to happen when similar great men meet. The proof of the catalysis is the first invention—which, despite its imperfection paves way for future invention. The first phase concludes with a successful fund-raising that resulted in Google becoming a public company.

(1)   Background: founders' birthplaces, childhood, and education: family and educational background are essential to the upbringing of great men because they provide the kind of environment that nurtures talents. The two founders' backgrounds are notedly ambivalent: on the one hand, the young Brin and Page do not have particularly remarkable upbringings. On the other hand, their parents have uncommon special talents.

Their history includes background information such as the founders' birth dates and places, parents' names and professions, and formal education. Both founders came from typical US middle-class families: the families were financially self-sufficient but not wealthy; the founders' parents had stable employment; and the founders went to the flagship universities of their home states before pursuing graduate studies at the prestigious Stanford University. The solid middle-classness of the founders reinforces an American belief that hard work, talent, and originality are key to success. The founders' upbringings easily resonate with readers and can inspire them—if Brin and Page can become wildly successful and fabulously rich, then the readers can as well.

Despite the emphasis on the founders' middle-classness, there are also unusual facts about the families' backgrounds. For example, Brin's childhood was typical among first- and second-generation immigrants, but his parents' mathematical talents are not skills that everyone has. *Astrum People* wrote, "the graduates of Soviet mathematics schools were highly valued worldwide. Therefore, it did not take much of the time for the head of the family to find a teaching position at the University of Maryland in College Park" (para. 8). Unlike the stereotypical image of immigrant parents working multiple low-paid, dead-end jobs, Brin's father moved up the professional ladder quickly once they arrived in the US. Brin's partner, Larry Page, also grew up with parents who were professors. They provided him with an environment that was atypical for an average family. Wikipedia quoted Page who said the childhood house "was usually a mess, with computers, science and technology magazines and *Popular Science* magazines all over the place" (para. 6).[2]

(2)   Partnership and mentorship: Brin and Page succeeded academically, having been admitted to the computer science PhD program at Stanford University. The history of Google often emphasized that Google would have been impossible without the synergy between Brin and Page. Yet, like a plot in a romance comedy, the founders were said to dislike each other at the very beginning. As *Wired* wrote, "It was hardly love at first sight. Walking up and down the city's hills [on the orientation] day, the two clashed incessantly, debating, among other things, the value of various approaches to urban planning. [...] Page recalls, [...] 'I thought he was pretty obnoxious. He had really strong opinions about things, and I guess I did, too'" (para. 2). However, in the expected plot that great minds are destined to be united, Page and Brin were said to become "intellectual soul-mates and close friends" (Wikipedia, para. 11). Mentors and peers of Brin and Page were mostly a passing interest in the founders' stories. Aside from their parents who were said to have taught them mathematics and fostered their intellectual development, the only other professor mentioned is Terry Winograd (Page's PhD adviser), primarily because he introduced the founders to one of the earliest Google investors Andy Bechtolsheim, a Stanford alumnus and co-founder of Sun Microsystems. No other fellow student or professor was said to matter to the intellectual growth of Brin and Page, making them appear to be the original inventors of data mining and web search algorithms.

(3)   First invention: what it is, how does it work, and why it is important? Google—the search engine—was presented as a completely original idea by the founders, even though technological invention requires scientists to stand on the shoulders of giants. The idea of indexing networked knowledge was dreamed of before the Internet was invented (Hillis, Petit, & Jarrett, 2013). The history decontextualized the earliest Google search engine from the body of scientific knowledge on which Brin and Page built their ideas. The history did not point out that the Internet provided a context in which a search engine could exist, conveniently ignoring the network as a history. In other words, if there had not been an exorbitant amount of online information, then a search engine would not have been necessary.

The creation of Google was literally said to be a eureka moment. Page's interest in studying web architecture was presented as an original—even divine—idea, that he just woke up one morning realizing the call, without any background research on the subject matter. For example, *Business Insider* wrote, "after Page suddenly woke up from a dream at 23 wondering if we could download the whole web, he started working on an idea to rank webpages" (para. 7).

The Google way of organizing information was implied to be a secret of nature that, once the founders had unlocked the secret, was able to profoundly change the way searches were done online. For example, the *Internet History Podcast* wrote, "Page was struck by a fundamental truth about the web that is glaringly obvious when you state it out loud: it is built on links. [...] But what occurred to Larry Page was that, as of yet, no one had bothered to analyze the structure of the link ecosystem in a comprehensive way" (para. 12). The *Internet History Podcast* further wrote, "it turned out that the reason search engines had never worked very well prior to PageRank [the former name of Google] was [...] because they were missing the key innovation that the [sic] Brin and Page had *stumbled* upon: relevancy" (para. 23; emphasis added).

Page and Brin said their method of ranking webpages was inspired by academic citations; the importance of an academic paper is evaluated by the number of times that it is cited in other papers. Even though the general public may not fully understand how academic citations work (a lot of under-graduate students certainly do not!) and Google's page rank is not exactly like academic citations, because the webpages do not go through a peer review process, the Google way of organizing information was said to be the best if not the only way. Google was not mentioned to be a search engine, among many competing ones, in the late 1990s.

(4)   Fund-raising and IPO: once the new search engine had gained popular-ity on the Stanford campus, the next step was for Brin and Page to look for investors. The ambivalent history is reinforced by the claim that the founders cared little about fundraising. The *Internet History Podcast* arti-cle said the founders only wanted investors who appreciated their work. Their meritocratic attitude was said to be as "supremely confident as ever" because "they didn't need anyone's help or money" (para. 52). The sites also described them to be reluctant entrepreneurs. Battelle (2005) wrote in *Wired* that neither of them were willing to drop out of the PhD program, they just gave Google a try. The history gave no reason why Brin and Page found it necessary to find investors. When it did, the reasons were comical rather than financial. A recurring story is that they hoarded every abandoned computer on campus. Then "they begged and borrowed Google into existence – a hard drive from the network lab, an idle CPU from the computer science loading docks" (Battelle, 2005, para. 22).

A few men were named to be the wise pioneers who saw the potential of Google: Andy Bechtolsheim of Sun Microsystems, Jeff Bezos of Amazon, and venture capital firms Kleiner Perkins Caufield & Byers and Sequoia Capital. However, the sites gave little information about what venture capital firms do, why they mushroomed in Silicon Valley during the dot-com boom, and how they are imperative to start-up hi-tech firms (see Chapter 4, "Political Profile"). Excite and Microsoft were said by many to be too unwise to pass up on the opportunity to acquire Google. The anecdote of the unwise shows the force of creative destruction, that, in capitalism, new technologies are bounded to destroy old technologies. In Google's tale, young but ambitious inventors like Brin and Page are said to have the intellect and guts to take over established technologies and upset the status quo. The sites implied that history would show that Excite became obsolete and largely forgotten; and Microsoft's search engine has little market search. (According to Net Marketshare.com, in late 2017 Microsoft's Bing only had about 8 percent search engine market shares while Google had 72 percent).

The first phase of the history of Google reinforces the myth of the American inventors: some clever youngsters waking up to a great idea, meeting a rival who turns out to be a trusting friend, and becoming accidentally successful. The history of Google on the websites was, however, full of ambivalence: the incorporation of Google was said to be a result of the founders' foresight, but they did not strive to be wealthy. Brin and Page were not pictured as strategic entrepreneurs who carefully plotted their moves; they followed few business conventions, yet managed to get ahead of the search engine market. At the conclusion of Phase 1, Page and Brin had very little choice: they were stuck in a position where they could no longer go back to finish their PhDs nor could they become employees of other companies. With much reluctance, they could only find investors, march ahead, and take the company public. The story did not explicate the capitalist context in which the founders developed their technology, yet it implied that capitalism made these circumstances possible.

Phase 2: Google as a Public Company

Google went public in August 2004. I chose the moment when it became a shareholder company as the beginning of the second phase. Becoming public connects Google to a wider network of capital (see Chapter 3, "Economic Profile") via the stock market. The wealth of the founders and the earliest employees is reflected in the minute by minute updates of the stock markets because they are the major individual stock owners. The primary theme in the second phase of the history of Google, as deduced from the sites, is expansion. Google was said to provide other search-related products and expanded its physical presence in Northern California. The company and owners also got involved in philanthropy to tackle issues that were not in the core business of online searches. The expansion was not always feasible because state control and public outcry stunted some development. The site did not explain why expansion was necessary in capitalism.

Not all online sites included every topic in the second phase (acquisitions; innovation and global expansion; philanthropy; controversies; physical plants); the information also tends to be disorganized. It is as if there was no prescribed way of how the second act of the story should unfold. Websites such as Biography.com and Britannica online that provide bare bone basic facts tend to include few topics in the second phase.

(5)   Acquisitions: there was no definition of what acquisition is, why Google had to do it, and why other companies were willing to be acquired. The ambivalence of the Google story continues: acquisition is a common business strategy but Google's unusual stance is emphasized. The Wikipedia page of Larry Page noted that Google "looked for usefulness above profitability, and long-term potential over near-term financial gains" (para. 37). The Sergey Brin page on *Famous People* offered an overly simplistic statement, saying the company "[became] one of the fastest growing internet companies in the world" (para. 2). Online websites only mentioned selected acquisitions and favored those that provide direct services for users such as YouTube. Lesser known services and backroom technologies were often omitted.

One theme in the second phase is the obsession with "bigness". Information about acquisitions is very often limited to the price that Google paid and how popular the services were prior to the acquisitions. Both implied that Google has an eye for good products and that they had the financial means to pay for the best. The best is seen as synonymous with "the most popular". Nothing is as blatant about Google's wealth and power as the one-line description under "evolving conglomerates" on the Larry Page page on Biography. com, "In 2006, Google purchased the most popular website for user-submitted streaming videos, YouTube, for $1.65 million in stock" (para. 5). The same fact was identically phrased in two other popular websites about Larry Page: Britannica online, and the Startup Stories "Larry Page biography" on YouTube. A similar sentiment about being big is expressed in Wikipedia, "In August 2011, Page announced that Google would spend $12.5 billion to acquire Motorola Mobility" (para. 39). Acquisition is treated like a shopping spree, with little explanation why it was essential for businesses.

(6)   Innovation and global expansion: information about new products and international expansion is also disorganized, with little explanation about why Google continued to innovate and expand globally. Descriptions of

new products created an illusion that innovation is in Google's genes and thus inevitable and natural. The only result of innovation was said to be financial success, "thanks to its innovation, the company is now one of the biggest brokers in the online advertising market" ("The History of Google" video). Innovation was also seen as being the same as a list of superlatives: "the *biggest*", "the *most* well known", "the *first* free webmail", and "the *first* e-mail service". In this logic, being innovative is synonymous with being the biggest and the first.

Moreover, online websites conflated all Google activities within a time period into one big laundry list, they neither explained the relationships between the activities nor suggested why some activities mattered more to Google's domination than others. For example, the History of Google page in Wikipedia listed in the first section, "Growth, 2003–2006", that Google had acquired Blogger; entered into partnership with NASA, Time Warner's AOL, and Sun Microsystems; discontinued the partnership with Yahoo!; become a verb in the dictionary; increased its market value; and intensified its rivalry with Microsoft. The second section "updates and evolution of ranking system" chronicles how webmasters "boost their SERP (search engine ranking position)" through using "deceitful SEO" to combat the practice of "splogging (the practice of creating nonsensical content to boost SERP of another site", "Googlebombing", etc.

Another instance to illustrate disorganized information came from InterestingEngineering.com, which charts Google's development at the turn of the century with a jumble of facts, "Google's defining characteristic of predictive search text had its origins in 2000 when MentalPlex was first deployed. This enabled Google to take part in Silicon Valley's tradition of April Fools' day hoaxes" (para. 21). It continued to list "millennial improvement" such as doodle series, multilingualism, international celebration (Bastille Day), an acquisition of Deja.com, Google Images, and an office in Tokyo.

While Google's motto is to organize the world's information, online sites about the history of Google seem to suffer from the problem of disorganized and decontextualized information; they do little to explain why Google innovates and expands to the global market; they also give the illusion that activities "just happened" without Google executives strategizing and planning.

(7) Philanthropy: similar to the previous two themes "acquisitions" and "innovation/global expansion", the sites offered little explanation as to why corporations launch foundations and how these non-profits traverse lobby issues that do not belong to the core business. Information about Google.org is listed at the very end, often treated as miscellaneous

tidbits. On Larry Page's biography Wikipedia page, Google.org is briefly mentioned under "other interests", which includes information such as the foundation's work in renewable energy technology, Page's investment in Tesla Motors, and "the socio-economic effects of advanced intelligent systems" (para. 50). The same nonspecific manner was used to talk about Google.org: under "personal life and legacy" of Sergey Brin's biography Wikipedia page, it was stated that "Sergey Brin and his ex-wife run the Brin Wojcicki Foundation, which donates money to various social causes" (para. 5). The Wikipedia page of Google has put the most effort into listing the achievements of Google.org: launched in 2004 with one billion dollars, its mission is "to create awareness about climate change, global public health, and global poverty" (para. 112). It also implied Google's stance in social issues such as gay marriage by mentioning the "legalize love" campaign.

(8)   Controversies: the history of Google was said to be mostly free of controversy. The Google Wikipedia page is one of the few sites that details the company's various bumps on the road. However, it states that criticisms (such as tax avoidance, search neutrality, copyright, censorship of search results, and privacy) are a result of Google's domination. Once again, there is a decontextualization of how the criticism also applies to other hi-tech companies, large and small. The site also mentioned Google's questionable business practices, such as "monopoly, restraint of trade, anti-competitive practices, and patent infringement" (para. 127). Lastly, it questioned whether the slogan "Don't be evil" was an empty saying or not. The online sites, however, gave few details on how Google resolved the controversies, the only kind mentioned being a lawsuit settlement.

(9)   Google campus and infrastructure: the quirkiness and perks of the Google campus were highlighted in both Google's official and unofficial sites: setting up shop, first in their dorm room, then moving to a garage, building a campus, and opening up international offices all happened within two decades. The expansion process illustrates the exorbitantly fast growth of the company. Its success in a competitive world is also reflected in the headquarters located in one of the most expensive real estate markets in the world. Despite the wealth of Google, the informal office atmosphere was highlighted to maintain the ambivalence of Google being highly successful but also unconventional. Nothing is more illustrative of this than the company's history page. Even though the official history page only has 444 words, a suitably titled "From the garage to the Googleplex" article ensures readers will know that the second office had "a clunky desktop computer, a ping-pong table, and

bright blue carpet". The fascination with objects was also illustrated on the Wikipedia page about the Googleplex lobby: "a piano, lava lamps, old server cluster" (para. 99).

The online sites are obsessed with the "bigness" of Google's offices. For example, the Wikipedia page stated that the sizes of the New York City and London offices are at 300,000 and 1 million square feet, respectively. Bigness is also shown from the high purchase price of the New York office ($1.9 billion), the number of international offices (70), and the number of countries in which Google has offices (40). Two other examples to show the websites' obsession with bigness, superlatives, and random facts are: (1) Googleplex's solar panels are the largest among US corporations; and (2) the use of goats to trim grass on the grounds of the headquarters.

The second phase of the history is unfocused: it mainly consists of scattered facts (in particular those that concern bigness) that do not constitute events that move the story forward. Also, few adversities were mentioned, leaving the readers unsure about how the actors changed after their trials and tribulations. From a narrative standpoint, the events appeared not to have causal relations and simply happened without any reason. Similar to the first phase, the broader political-economic context was conveniently ignored in the second phase. Since the capitalist nature of Google is not taken into account, business strategies such as acquisitions, global expansion, and innovation reinforce the ambivalent attitude of Brin and Page when they first founded the company: that great ideas will not be ignored even if they are implemented without much business planning.

Phase 3: Alphabet

(10) Restructuring: on 10th August, 2015, Page announced the establishment of Alphabet, which became the parent company of Google. Online sites continued to fuel the ambivalence of the history of Google. On the online sites, the dramatic move was only briefly mentioned, using information drawn from Page's letter on the Alphabet website, which contains less than basic information: this $90-billion company only has a one-page official webpage with a less than 1,000-word description, one link to a subsidy, and an image of a few wooden blocks. Although Google is an information organizer and although Page wrote that the company would improve transparency, what Alphabet is and does—as reflected on the website—seems to be highly secretive and opaque. (More on the technology conglomerate in Chapter 3, "Economic Profile"). From a narrative perspective, the third phase is definitely not signaled as the ending chapter of Google because the search company continues to thrive in

terms of revenue. But it is unclear how the second phase led to the third phase: what events drove the story of Google, and who drove the events and the evaluations of these events?

Network Analysis

The narrative analysis above is effective at showing how online sites tell the story of Google history. However, some may object that a narrative analysis is biased because of its interpretive nature; that the researcher—self-identified as a political economist—brought in her own experience and worldview into delineating the story of the history of Google. In order to remedy the shortcoming, I employed network analysis to quantify information by counting the most common keywords on webpages about Google history. Network analysis provides an objective result of social relations because it quantifies, describes, and predicts them. It has been applied to understand networks of co-authorship by using Google Scholars data (some examples are Harzing & Wal, 2008; Matveeva & Poldin, 2016).

I used the phrase "history of Google" on Google Search to gather links to webpages displayed on the first five pages of search results. I chose five because Google Search prides itself on providing an objective ranking that shows the most relevant results on the first few pages. It believes that there is no reason why users should linger on the search results pages. Users who ask a broad question such as "history of Google" may find the first five pages of search results to be sufficient. Using this procedure, 45 websites were gathered.

The second step was to "scrape" words, phrases, and sentences with hyperlinks from the body text of the webpages. Scraping refers to the computational process of extracting the text from a collection of webpages (Ignatow & Mihalcea, 2017). I used two software programs, Octoparse and Outwit, for the scraping. Hyperlinks are seen as "votes" by Google; relevant websites are seen as those linked by others (Halavais, 2009).

For all the webpages, I chose the body text to scrape because of two reasons: first, the body text contains content that addresses the history of Google; second, the body text contains links that connect to other webpages on which more relevant information can be found. I ignored components such as publication title, article title, author's name, table of contents, side bars (such as "see also"), and links to relevant articles, endnotes, and advertisements.

For example, the first paragraph of the body text about the history of Google on Wikipedia is:

> The Google company was officially launched in 1998 by Larry Page and Sergey Brin to market Google Search, which has become the most widely used web-based search engine. Page and Brin, students at

Stanford University in California, developed a search algorithm at first known as "BackRub" in 1996. The search engine soon proved successful and the expanding company moved several times, finally settling at Mountain View in 2003. This marked a phase of rapid growth, with the company making its initial public offering in 2004 and quickly becoming one of the world's largest media companies. The company launched Google News in 2002, Gmail in 2004, Google Maps in 2005, Google Chrome in 2008, and the social network known as Google+ in 2011, in addition to many other products. In 2015, Google became the main subsidiary of the holding company Alphabet Inc.[3]

The keywords that were scraped from the first paragraph are the hyperlinked words: "Google", "Larry Page", "Sergey Brin", "Google Search", "web-based search engine", "Stanford University", "Mountain View", "initial public offering", "Google News", "Gmail", "Google Maps", "Google Chrome", "social network", "Google+", "many other products", "Alphabet Inc". The scraped texts were saved into an Excel file and the keywords were manually checked against the links on the original webpages. Wrong or missed keywords/phrases/sentences were corrected or added.

The next step was data cleaning. First, I standardized one speech form because I was more interested in the semantic meanings than the form of speech. For example, "Google announced" and "the announcement made by Google" were seen as semantically identical because the keyword is "announced". Second, I determined what the keyword(s) is/are when a link has more than one word (such as sentences and phrases). For example, the keyword in the phrase "algorithms that rank results" was determined to be "algorithms". Some phrases or sentences have more than one keyword. For example, in the phrase "by combining data and intuition", I determined the keywords to be "data" and "intuition".

After cleaning up the data, I singled out words that appeared five or more times. The occurrence and frequency of keywords inform at a global level what readers are supposed to know about the history of Google. In all the webpages, 45 keywords appeared 5 or more times. These keywords were used for the network analysis. If I also included keywords that appeared 4 times, there would be an additional 17 keywords, which would cluster the network illustration. Therefore, while the decision between five and four was arbitrary, I gave consideration to the meaningfulness and clarity of the data represented in Figure 2.1. While keywords that appeared four times would also give information about the history of Google, 62 keywords would have clustered the network illustration, making it harder to differentiate keywords that give the most information from those that give less.

To build the network, I used two kinds of nodes: "keyword" and "site". In the terminology of network analysis, a node can be a person, an organization,

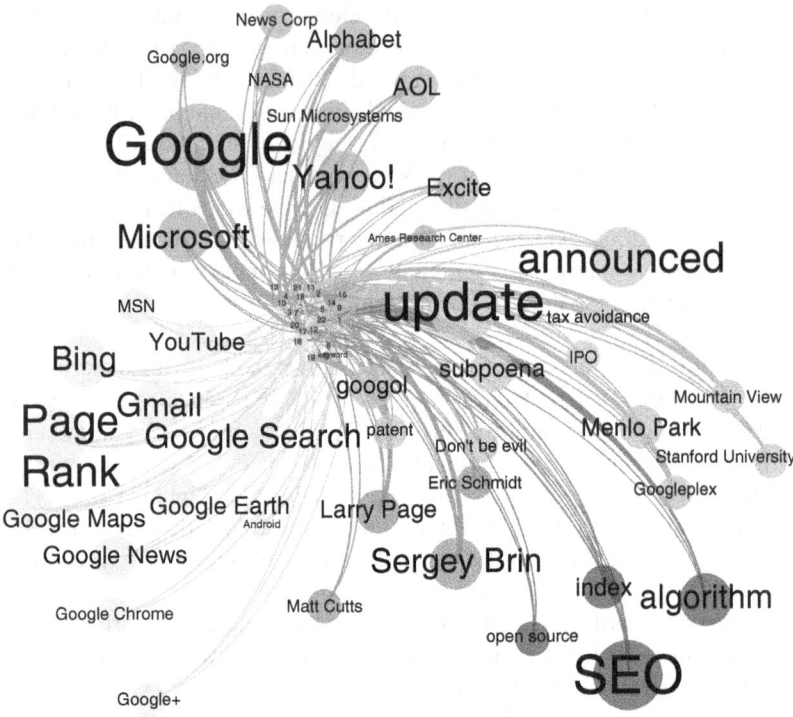

Figure 2.1 Network of Keywords on Webpages about the "History of Google".

a URL, and so on. I have suggested how "keyword" was selected in the previous paragraph. As for "site", I omitted sites that had no links in the body text and those that did not have any keywords, because such sites did not have any relation with the keywords. Among the 45 sites on the first 5 pages of search results, only 22 remained after the elimination.

The keywords and sites were categorized into different types, each type is represented on the network. The types are: "action" (action verbs), "app" (applications and software programs associated with a company), "org" (organizations, including for profit companies, non-profit organizations, and government agencies), "mis" (miscellaneous items), "site" (the webpages from where the keywords were scraped), "people", "place" (geographical locations), and "tech" (technologies that are not exclusively owned by one company, such as the Internet). In the software program Gephi, I used sites as the source and keywords as the target. I established the relationship between the source and the target by seeing the sites as the nodes that initiate the relations. In other words, the webpages took the initiative to decide what keywords could be used to write about the history of Google. The keywords, on the other hand, could not decide on which webpages they would appear.

As seen in Figure 2.1, the tiny nodes in the center represent the sources (i.e., the websites where the keywords came from). The targets (i.e., keywords on the websites) are represented by the nodes radiated from the center. Each of the targets is connected to the sources by the curved lines whose thickness denotes the number of sites that contain the keywords: the thicker the lines are, the more websites have the same keywords. The bigger the circles and font size are, the more common the keywords are on the website.

The following summarizes what Google Search tells us about the history of Google from a network perspective:

- Applications played the most important role in the history of Google because they were mentioned the most and there are more "app" nodes than other types of nodes (such as place, people, etc.). The majority of the applications are Google's own (PageRank, Google+, Gmail, Google News, Google Chrome, Google Maps, YouTube, Google Search, and Google Earth). The only two applications that played a role in the history but not owned by the company are MSN and Bing, both owned by Microsoft. Not all Google applications were seen to play an equal role. Those related to search—PageRank (the algorithm) and Google Search (the application)—were seen to be the most important. YouTube and Gmail are the next important applications in the history.

- Organizations were also seen to play a key role in the history of Google, only second to applications. Yahoo! and Excite, two companies that offer Internet search services, as well as Microsoft, were seen to play a more important role than AOL and Sun Microsystems. Google's parent company, Alphabet, and the philanthropy arm Google.org were mentioned but neither appeared as prominently as Google(.com).

- Few people and places were seen to be important in the history of Google: Only four people were seen to play an important role (the two founders Larry Page and Sergey Brin; the first CEO Eric Schmidt; and a former web spam engineer Matt Cutts). The only places that mattered in the history of Google are all in California and within a few miles of each other: radiating from Stanford University are Menlo Park (where Google had the first office in a garage) and Mountain View (where Googleplex, Alphabet's headquarters, is located).

- Few action verbs were associated with the history of Google. Four among the five were actions initiated by Google: "announced", "update", "IPO" (initial public offering), and "tax avoidance". Only one node was an action done to Google: "subpoena".

- Among all keywords, the five that appeared the most and were mentioned in the most websites were: Google, update, algorithm, Sergey Brin, and Larry Page. The other five keywords that frequently appeared but were not mentioned in most websites were: Microsoft, Yahoo!, announced, SEO, and PageRank. Some websites overwhelmingly used certain keywords (such as "announced"), making them appear prominent.
- Most of the keywords came from a small number of websites: 244 out of 412 keywords came from three sites only: Wikipedia pages of Google and the History of Google, and the Wikiwand page of the History of Google. Twelve websites have fewer than five keywords.

How Does Network Analysis Add to Narrative Analysis?

A network analysis of the keywords gathered from webpages on the history of Google reinforces a few findings from the narrative analysis. First, only a few people mattered in the history of Google. Second, the history of Google is ahistorical and devoid of a political-economic context. Third, Google is mainly a search engine.

There are fewer nodes of "people" than of organizations and applications in the network: the two founders, the first CEO, and a former spam engineer were the only four people who mattered in a company of 85,000 (as of July 2018). Fuchs (2011) critiqued popular studies of Google for ignoring employees' labor and the role of venture capital in the development of Google. The few prominent names in the network confirm this claim. From all the webpages, an addition of five people were mentioned more than once: Andy Bechtolsheim (the first investor), Danny Sullivan (a journalist who now works for Google), Sundar Pichai (current CEO), Terry Winograd (PhD advisor of Page), and Susan Wojcicki (CEO of YouTube, one of the first few employees). The handful of people mentioned in the history of Google reinforces an American technology myth that it only takes a genius (or two) to invent technologies that transform the world. This myth is best illustrated by Thomas Edison, often known as the greatest inventor; many images only show him and his inventions, but few show his workshop of hired workers. Invention was treated as a eureka moment in the history of Google, it was not seen as a result of knowledge accumulation. Even though Brin and Page wrote the PageRank algorithm by building upon existing knowledge, both narrative analysis and network analysis suggest that those who had worked on Internet search before the founders did not matter much in Google's history.

A network analysis of keywords also shows that the history of Google is devoid of a historical political-economic context. Indeed the history of Google is not really about the past but the present. In all the webpages, the action verb "founded" only appeared once while "announced" appeared 8 times and "updates" 34. The nodes of organizations show that the only two organizations that mattered in the history of Google are Yahoo! and Excite. The network does not contain keywords about the earliest Internet such as ARPANET or pre-Internet knowledge categorization systems such as a library catalog or encyclopedia. The network analysis shows that, geographically, the history of Google is intensely localized, the only four places that mattered to the history are Google's various headquarters in northern California. The state and country where the Google headquarters is located are less important than the places local to it: "California" appeared only three times and the "U.S." once! Even though Google relies on many workers in different countries and the many more users living in dispersed locales around the globe, only the headquarter location(s) mattered. The intensely "local" places associated with Google reinforces a myth that Google could have existed anywhere but it just *happened* to begin at Stanford University. The history conveniently ignores the fact that the university pushes its faculty and students to monetize their inventions (see Chapter 3, "Economic Profile"). This further adds to the ambivalence of the history of Google: Page and Brin had both an unusual *and* an ordinary childhood; they had a good idea *and* a not-too-serious-attitude toward business; Google can be anywhere in the world *and* it is in northern California.

Lastly, the narrative and network analysis show that Google is still primarily seen as a search engine. The narrative analysis shows that the most coherent storyline is the invention of Google Search. Once Google became a public company, the history became unfocused and disorganized. Similarly, the network analysis shows that the most common nodes are all related to search: PageRank, Google Search, and Bing. Network analysis, however, shows that a few known applications were also important in the history of Google: Gmail, Google Earth, Google News, and Google Chrome. Both narrative analysis and network analysis are relatively mute about the businesses owned by Alphabet, the parent company. Keywords such as venture capital, biotechnology, equity investment, data carrier, and automobile were not common in the webpages.

Network analysis adds to narrative analysis by giving empirical evidence to support findings from an interpretative analysis. Network analysis, however, is not sufficient to capture the semantic meanings of the websites' body text for two reasons: first, some authors used generic words such as "updates" or "this" as links. These words as texts are not informative about the history of Google. Second, the body texts of 17 webpages did not have any links at all, so those webpages were omitted from the analysis. This begs the question of whether hyperlinked texts are necessarily keywords and whether it is possible to identify keywords that have no hyperlinks.

How is Network Analysis Useful to Political Economists?

The ontology of the political economy of communication is grounded in realism (Mosco, 2009). As such, political economists, in principle, do not object to the use of empirical data; this is particularly the case for financial data. Nevertheless, since the use of quantitative research methods and empirical data in the US, academia has long been associated with positivist social science, and political economists are critical of the assumption that empirical data reflect social relations in reality. Because political economists aim to unveil how power operates in and through social actors and institutions, they do not believe that a positivist stance will reveal what the reality is. Therefore, even though the above network analysis has demonstrated that computational methods such as text mining and network analysis are useful at quantitatively measuring keyword occurrences and deducing relationships between keywords and webpages, political economists should critique—not accept—the network of keywords reflecting a "reality", because webpages are cultural technological artifacts co-created by algorithm and content providers. Both actors are highly aware of the political-economic implications of webpage relevance and hyperlinks.

Webpages are cultural technological artifacts, they are actively and inter-subjectively shaped by both non-human (algorithm) and human actors (e.g., software engineers, content providers). Software and hardware both restrict and enable how an algorithm is written, how webpages are developed, and how digital information is retrieved. Humans create artifacts that are deemed culturally useful and meaningful. For example, the search engine that locates the most relevant information, or webpages that describe the history of a company. However, these cultural artifacts need to be situated in a political-economic context. In this case, webpages were written not because they provided new, relevant, and meaningful information, but because they were spaces that contained paid content.

To answer the question "what is Google?", the story of Google history is not even so much about the narrative and the keywords, it is about the human–non-human network that co-creates such cultural artifacts. In other words, to future generations, what is interesting about online culture circa 2019 may not be the history of Google, but how the search results illustrate human–machine interaction. If the network does not survive but the artifacts do, future generations who study historical online culture may find it puzzling why this generation produced webpages with content that is so similar. Future generations may also wonder why there is such a huge variety among the most relevant webpages: while the most relevant page from Wikipedia has 74 links and close to 34,000 words, the fourth most relevant webpage from Thoughtco.com only has 4 links and 800 words. They might also wonder why there was such a huge variation in the number of display ads: while there is no ad on the Wikipedia page, the Thoughtco.com page has 8 prominent ads: 1 drops down from the top, 2 large and 2 small on the side bar, 3 at the bottom (including 1 with a moving image), as well as 15 "suggested" articles (each with an image). Future generations may find that cultural artifacts tell very little about the *becoming* of Google, but the network tells a lot. If future generations discover how the Google algorithm worked, and how and why content providers responded to it, they will understand why the cultural artifacts shared certain qualities. They may also understand that, by being in a network, content providers took up the attribute of the network and acted upon what the algorithm deemed relevant (Callon, 1999; Latour, 2005).

Notes

1 *How Search Works. Google Search.* www.google.com/search/howsearchworks/. Accessed 20th July, 2018.
2 The Wikipedia citation is incorrect. The quote was mistakenly said to come from page's founders' letter in the 2013 Google annual report.
3 *History of Google.* Wikipedia. https://en.wikipedia.org/wiki/History_of_Google. Accessed: 9th January, 2019.

Bibliography

Akinsanya, A. & Bach, C. (2014, April). Narrative analysis: The personal experience narrative approach. Paper presented at ASEE Zone I Conference. University of Bridgeport, CT, USA.

Battelle, J. (2005). *The search: How Google and its rivals rewrote the rules of businesses and transformed our culture.* New York: Portfolio.

Callon, M. (1999). Actor-network theory: The market test. In: J. Law & J. Hassard (Eds.), *Actor network theory and after* (pp. 181–195). Oxford, UK: Blackwell.

Fuchs, C. (2011). A contribution of the critique of the political economy of Google. *Fast Capitalism, 8*(1). Retrieved from: www.uta.edu/huma/agger/fastcapitalism/8_1/fuchs8_1.html. Accessed: 2nd April, 2019.

Halavais, A. (2009). *Search engine society.* Cambridge, UK: Polity.

Harzing, A. W., & van der Wal, R. (2008). Google Scholar as a new source for citation analysis? *Ethics in Science and Environmental Politics, 8*(1), 61–73.

Hillis, K., Petit, M., & Jarrett, K. (Eds.). (2013). *Google and the culture of search.* New York: Routledge.

Ignatow, G., & Mihalcea, R. (2017). *Text mining: A guidebook for the social sciences.* Thousand Oaks, CA: Sage.

Jeanneney, J.-N. (2007). *Google and the myth of universal knowledge.* Chicago, IL: University of Chicago Press.

Jovchelovitch, S., & Bauer, M. W. (2000). Narrative interviewing. In: M. W. Bauer & G. Gaskell (Eds.), *Qualitative researching with text, image and sound: A practical handbook* (pp. 57–74). London: Sage.

Latour, B. (2005). *Reassembling the social: An introduction to actor-network theory*. Oxford, UK: Oxford University Press.

Matveeva, N., & Poldin, O. (2016). Citation of scholars in co-authorship network: Analysis of Google Scholar data. *Applied Econometrics*, *44*, 100–118.

Mosco, V. (2009). *The political economy of communication* (2nd ed.). London: Sage.

Segev, E. (2010). *Google and the digital divide: The bias of online knowledge*. Oxford, UK: Chandos.

Vaidhyanathan, S. (2011). *The googlization of everything (And why we should worry)*. Berkeley, CA: University of California Press.

Yang, S., Keller, F. B., & Zheng, L. (2017). *Social network analysis: Methods and examples*. Los Angeles, CA: Sage.

3   Economic Profile

This chapter will focus on Alphabet when it was founded in 2015 as the parent company of Google. Alphabet is not seen as a *new* company in this book, but as a continuation of Google. From a network perspective, Alphabet reconfigured itself by grouping all Internet businesses under the company Google. Previous units and divisions that were seen as non-Internet-centric were dissociated from Google. These units and divisions became independently financed and managed under Alphabet. While I will summarize my previous work in this chapter, readers who are interested in a more detailed account of the economic profile of pre-Alphabet Google may want to consult Lee (2010) and Lee (2016).

In this chapter, I situate the economic profile of Alphabet in the network of capital. Alphabet and other hi-tech companies have brought forth a networked economy that maximizes the flow of capital. By this I mean three things: first, Alphabet's economy relies on the Internet. Without the Internet as an infrastructure, Alphabet and other hi-tech companies would not have existed. This point has been made in Chapter 1, "Introduction", and Chapter 2, "History".

Second, the economic activities of Alphabet take place within a commercialized Internet. Despite Alphabet's business plan to diversify the company to industries such as biotechnology and self-driving cars, the majority of the company's revenue still comes from online advertising. Ad buying and ad viewing on Google are solely done online. Ad buyers are asked to bid for keywords online; the ads shown next to search results lure users to view and hopefully click on them. Beyond online advertising, Alphabet also ventures into distributing media goods to diversify revenue. The media store, Google Play, however, does not sell hard copies of books, CDs, and DVDs, it only offers online media streaming and electronic books.

Third, this networked economy is capitalistic and historical. Technology does not evolve in a political-economic vacuum; the political-economic context in which technology is invented constrains how it is developed.

As the great grand narrative of Internet history tells us, the Internet was conceived in the military before it was developed by computer enthusiasts who envisioned it being a decentralized communication network free from government control. The economy of the earliest Internet was not perceived in capitalistic terms, even though the broader economy in which the Internet was developed is predominately capitalistic. Similarly, when Brin and Page first conceived the concept of a search engine with objective results, they saw it as a mathematical problem than an economic problem. However, economic constraints such as limited funds hindered the founders' ability to buy hardware, and they had to think like capitalists in order to continue the projects. Their PhD institution, Stanford University, also steers inventors to become entrepreneurs by promoting commercialization of technology among faculty and students. According to the Office of Technology Licensing (OTL),

> OTL receives invention disclosures from Stanford faculty, staff and students. We evaluate these disclosures for their commercial possibilities, and when possible license them to industry. If the inventions are successfully licensed, cash royalties collected by OTL provide funding to the inventors' departments and schools, as well as personal shares for the inventors themselves.[1]

If Google's search engine had been developed in another context or another society, the economy of the search engine would have been different. However, at present, it is almost impossible to think how a non-capitalistic networked economy might look, given the majority of activities on the Internet are conducted on commercial sites.

Time in a Capitalistic Networked Economy

The commercialization of the Internet reconfigures how time is perceived. I argue in this chapter that the economies of Google and Alphabet are based on the promise of an infinite expansion of time. Because the majority of Alphabet's revenue comes from online advertising, the company has to expand the time that users spend online and to expand the number of users. Alphabet's non-Internet-centric businesses were set up to assist Google to infinitely expand time. In the following, I examine how time in capitalism has been studied.

Marx (1867/1887) saw the circulation of capital as a problem of time. Capital commodifies time by assigning a value to it. Workers who sell their labor-power to capitalists no longer own the time. The market objectifies time by measuring the value generated by labor in a market. In a working day, workers labor for a fraction of time to produce commodities that bear an exchange value; this value is *necessary* for the workers to sustain their lives. For another fraction of time, workers labor to produce surplus value for the capitalists. The surplus value is reallocated to the production cycle so that more raw materials and labor can be purchased.

Capital has to continuously circulate itself to produce more surplus value. The cycle of surplus reallocation cannot be broken or slowed down because "capital is dead labor, that, vampire-like, only lives by sucking living labor, and lives the more, the more labor it sucks" (Marx, 1867/1887, p. 163). Capital that shrinks or removes from circulation is seen to hurt the economy. For example, investment that has no return or negative return, or money stacked away in a cupboard, are seen as unwise money management.

Time also relates to the realization of value. Once a commodity is produced for the market, it has a certain timeframe to leave the shelves before it becomes valueless. This applies to fresh fruit in a supermarket as much as Christmas decorations after the holidays have finished. When a product is being purchased, the capitalist pockets both the capital that was used to produce the commodity and the profits made through the purchase. The faster the product is sold, the faster the process of value realization is.

How does a networked economy realize Marx's conceptualization of time? How does the network assist circulation of capital? I argue that Google's search engine appears to create infinite time by creating multiple spaces at once. The appearance of infinite time and multiple spaces creates an illusion that capital can seamlessly flow through multiple spaces where time is no longer constrained by 24 hours in a day and 60 minutes in an hour.

A search engine, on the surface, can overcome the temporal and spatial limits of capital. For one thing, the Internet is believed to make space irrelevant. Consumers are no longer constrained by their local locations, they can easily shop in an online store located in their town, as well as one on the other side of the globe. For another thing, the Internet is also believed to make time irrelevant: consumers can buy anything at any time online; and a large number of online users can visit a large number of websites at any given time. The multiple spaces and simultaneous commercial activities online create an infinite timeframe for users. Both conditions are ideal for advertisers, because their advertisements are no longer constrained by the hours that television runs or the number of pages printed in a publication, advertisements can appear in as many search results as possible (Lee, 2011).

Nonetheless, online advertising is still constrained by the number of users and the waking hours of these users during which they can go online. Even though Google.com is the most visited website in the entire world, it has to continually expand time and space in order to continuously produce surplus value. Alphabet's solution is thus to increase the number of online users and also to increase the time that users spend on Alphabet's products.

The company's ambition is reflected from Page who wrote, in an optimistic tone, that despite Google's core products generating one billion monthly active users (Alphabet, 2015), "we are just beginning to scratch the surface" (p. 2). This ambiguous sentence may mean Alphabet will increase the number of users infinitely through Google and non-Internet businesses. Page's optimism is not unsupported. According to the International Telecommunication Union (ITU), only half of the world population had access to the Internet in 2018. In the least connected nations, only one in five individuals is connected (International Telecommunication Union, 2018). So, Alphabet prides itself with providing Internet connection to these unconnected populations.

Another reason why Page should be optimistic is because mobile technology will be the predominant means of accessing the Internet, especially among populations in developing countries. Alphabet , therefore, needs to ensure its mobile platform will dominate the market by partnering with hardware manufacturers, or becoming one itself. Time and space are created once a consumer uses Alphabet products and services.

In the context of an expansion of infinite time, I discuss in the following if the founding of the parent company, Alphabet, is indeed a new development of Google, then I will look at the corporate structure and properties of this new parent company. Afterward, I examine the financial data to show that Alphabet is still a search company and its main revenue still comes from online advertising. The markets in which Alphabet operates are not hugely competitive because they are shared by only a few corporations. Lastly, Alphabet stays competitive in these markets by aggressive acquisition and a huge research and development (R&D) budget.

New Developments? From G(oogle) to A(lphabet)

In October 2015, Larry Page announced that, together with Brin, he had founded a new company called Alphabet. In a very short letter to the public and investors, Page explained why they founded this new company: "we've long believed that over time companies tend to get comfortable doing the same thing [... , but] in the technology industry, where revolutionary ideas drive the next big growth areas, you need to be uncomfortable to stay relevant" (Page, 2015, para. 3). The founding of Alphabet reinforces the belief that technology is forward-looking, and evolves in a breakneck speed, and that any company that does not constantly invent technologies will quickly become obsolete. The founding of Alphabet also illustrates the ideas of creative destruction and disruptive technologies. Creative destruction harbors the belief that technology does not simply build and improve upon older technology, but technology always breaks new ground and ultimately destroys existing technologies. Disruptive technologies are said to bring a new order to the existing one by erasing old social, political, economic, and cultural practices. Page believed in creative destruction and disruptive technology by suggesting that those who do not dream big and sit on their laurels would soon find their companies failing. Page and Brin believed that when their time was freed up by not being wholly involved in running Google, they could "continue to scale out aspirations" (para. 7) and "[be] in the business of starting new things" (para. 8).

Page (2015) continued to explain that Alphabet is a *collection* of companies in which Google is still the crown jewel. However, businesses that are not closely related to Internet services and products will be removed from Google and owned by Alphabet. Some of these businesses, which are grouped under Alphabet, not Google, are venture capital firms, drone delivery services, healthcare products, self-driving cars, clean energy, and so on. Page continued to suggest that Alphabet is not interested in being a consumer brand with related products, so each of its companies should have its own distinctive brands and independence. Page's letter neither named all of Alphabet's companies nor did it name the industries to which Alphabet was expanding. It is unknown if the omission was intended to make the new company appear mysterious or to avoid Alphabet being perceived as a conglomerate.

What is the goal of the new company Alphabet? Apparently, making more profits, expanding to more markets, reaching out to more consumers, and eliminating competition are not some of the stated goals. The goals, according to Page (2015), are more noble:

- Getting more ambitious things done.
- Taking the long-term view.
- Empowering great entrepreneurs and companies to flourish.
- Investing at the scale of the opportunities and resources we see.
- Improving the transparency and oversight of what we're doing.
- Making Google even better through greater focus.
- And hopefully … as a result of all this, improving the lives of as many people as we can.

(para. 11)

The new development, Alphabet, was intended, thus, not to replace the ideals of Google (i.e., organize the world's information) but to strengthen its ideals, because Google had been conceptualized with the grand ambition of bettering humankind with better access to information. Alphabet also wanted to spread its ideals to other companies and entrepreneurs through investment.

Corporate Structure and Properties

In 2015, after filing with the US Securities and Exchange Commission (SEC), Alphabet reinforced that it is a collection of businesses: while Google is the largest, it also includes Verily, Calico, X, Nest, GV, Google Capital, and Google Fiber (more on all these companies later in the chapter). These non-Google businesses are collectively called "Other Bets". While the name "Other Bets" is tongue-in-cheek, it also has a grain of truth because they are not yet proven to be profit-making. When Alphabet was formed in 2015, only 0.6 percent of the revenue came from non-Google businesses, however, this has increased to 1 percent in 2017 (Alphabet, 2017). In terms of real money, the revenue has increased fourfold in two years from $445 million to $1,203 million.

Google's Core Businesses

Although Google is still seen as a search company (see Chapter 2, "History"), its core businesses encompass all aspects of the Internet, from software to hardware, and from consumer services to business solutions. Its 10K report suggested that the core businesses of Google are in Ads, Android, Chrome, Commerce, Google Cloud, Google Maps, Google Play, Hardware, Search, and YouTube. These products undoubtedly require no introduction to regular Internet users around the globe.

Google Search services dominate the online world. According to Alexa. com, Google.com (aka Google Search) is the most visited website around the globe as of December 2018.[2] An average user spends about 7 and 36 seconds a day on Google Search. An average visitor looked at slightly more than nine unique pages on Google Search. The second most visited website is YouTube.com, also owned by Google. While an average of eight minutes was spent on YouTube.com per user per day, the average user looked at fewer unique pages. In addition to Google.com, regional sites from India, Japan, Hong Kong, Brazil, Russia, the UK, Germany, and France were also among the most visited top 50 websites around the globe in December 2018.

Are Gmail, Google Maps, and Google Play about search? These online services for consumers may be more than search services, yet Google believes that the core of these services are about storing and retrieving information. For example, Gmail was designed with a "search" mindset. While Bill Gates questioned why e-mail users would need huge storage, Brin and Page see the inbox as a database where all e-mails are stored. Gmail was then designed to make information retrieval convenient (Levy, 2011). Google Play may appear like an online media store by offering movie and television streaming, audiobooks, e-books, and apps to download. But search is also at the heart of

Google Play because keywords are used to search for products across media. For example, when the keyword "Google" is used on Google Play, it shows Google apps, audiobooks, and ebooks related to Google, as well as movies and music (even though none of the titles are about Google).

Beyond searches, Google also offers an operating system and software for consumers: the Chrome browser, the Android mobile operating system, and Google Docs are some of these services. Beyond free online services for consumers, Google provides solutions to businesses. According to Alphabet 10K report (Alphabet, 2017), Google provides businesses with infrastructure, security, data management, analytics, and artificial intelligence. Its cloud services (Google Cloud Platform and G Suite) are geared toward business customers.

Google has moved beyond software by entering into hardware markets such as smartphone (Google Pixel), tablet (Pixel Slate), and laptop (Pixelbook). It has also moved into smart home technologies by selling voice a recognition "assistant", speakers, and routers. Last, but not least, it also sells virtual reality goggles.

Google's core business is indeed dazzling but all the services and products can still be reduced down to one thing: information. More precisely, how Google offers "free" services in exchange for information. As I argued elsewhere (Lee, 2010, 2011), Google vertically integrated its online services and advertising services. On the users' side, in order to enjoy the "free" services offered by Google (such as Search, YouTube, Google Maps, Gmail), they have to be shown ads. Even if the ads are said to be relevant to users, the ads are still commercial messages paid by advertisers who want users to become consumers. On the advertisers' side, in order to pay a right price to reach the customers, they have to play by Google's advertising rules (they will be explained in the "major revenue" section). Google's ability to invent a dominant online advertising market is due to its capability of amassing information. Because Google knows the most popular keywords used for search, it has the knowledge to set a price for keywords to be bid.

By creating the online advertising system, Google expands time and space for both the users and advertisers. Traditional advertising is constrained by time and space: a television commercial only runs for a certain duration, a newspaper ad can only occupy a certain space. But the Internet seems to expand both space and time by making both infinite: the more searches are done online, the more search results are generated; the more search results are generated, the more ads are shown; the more ads are shown, the more time will be spent on looking at ads. The problem, then, is to *infinitely* create more users. One way to do so is to vertically integrate hardware and software.

Google's move to hardware may not be surprising given its insatiable hunger to expand its markets and users. Unlike Apple that began in the hardware market and then moved to software, Google went the opposite direction. Google phone, tablet, laptop, and home assistant system are pre-programmed with Google software that comes with various search functions. For example, Google phone is pre-programmed with the Android operating system, Google Assistant (an artificial intelligence voice recognition and command application), and an array of Google apps (Google Maps, YouTube, Gmail, Chrome browser, Google Photos, Google Play, Google News, and Google Drive). Similar to two of the most popular phones in the US, Apple phone and Samsung Galaxy, Google phones lock in hardware and software: users cannot install an Apple operating system on a Google phone, or vice versa.

Alphabet probably does not aim to dramatically increase revenue by selling hardware, but it aims to increase the number of Android users. It is evident that the Google phone, Pixel, is hardly a competitive player in the crowded market. In the first 9 months in 2017, the majority of the smartphone market in the US was shared by Apple (31 percent), Samsung (26 percent), LG (17 percent), and ZTE (11 percent). Pixel only has 1 percent of the market (Gallagher, 2018). It is unknown how many units of Google phone have been sold, because Alphabet did not report it. On the surface, Alphabet appears to be wasting resources in order to develop hardware in an already crowded field, this is particularly the case when the hardware market is one where economies of scale are important. However, if hardware is a means by which Google can increase the market share of the Android operating system, then Pixel does not need to outsell its chief competitor Apple in order to increase the market share of Android, because Android is already the most popular operating system on mobile phones. Even if Google's Pixel has only a few percent of market shares, Android will maintain its dominant position in the smartphone market. Since Google needs to *infinitely* increase the time spent on Google Search services, a small increase of its shares may not be insignificant.

"Other Bets"

Non-Google businesses in Alphabet include: Verily, Calico, X, Nest, GV, CapitalG, and Google Fiber. Each of these businesses has its own CEO and is independently financed and managed. Some businesses were developed in-house in the pre-Alphabet Google era (such as Verily), others were acquired (such as Nest). Some businesses use the Google brand (such as Google Capital), but others stray away from it (such as Calico). Even though Google aims to organize the world's information, non-Google businesses that do not provide consumer technology tend to provide very little information about what they do. The following section outlines some of the businesses that fall under "Other Bets" and what they do.

X (formerly Google X): an innovation lab that began in 2010 in the pre-Alphabet Google era. X was tasked to work on hard, long-term "moonshot" problems. It works on some of the technologies that have generated much press, such as self-driving cars, Google Glass, stratospheric balloons, energy kites, drone technology, carbon emissions deduction, and cybersecurity. The mission of X reflects the founders' ambitions to do things on a grand scale. Its mission is to "create radical new technologies to solve some of the world's hardest problems".[3] It aims to lift up the lives of billions of people and create ten times the impact on the world's most challenging problems. But all those problems are, unsurprisingly, technological and have the potential to be commercialized, such as delivering the Internet to rural areas and delivering goods by drones. Although X sounds like a place where "crazy" ideas are tested, it is expected that the innovations do "graduate" (in X's term) and become standalone companies under Alphabet, such as Verily and Chronicle (see later).

Verily Life Sciences: a health data company spin-off from Google X. The three main types of projects are: (1) providing tools and platforms to make healthcare decisions and interventions; (2) predicting and preventing the spread of disease; and (3) changing how healthcare is delivered.[4]

Calico: a research and development company that seeks an understanding of the biology that controls lifespan.[5]

Nest: smart home technologies company. It sells energy-conversing products such as a programmable thermostats with built-in artificial intelligence; home security technologies such as security cameras, video doorbells, alarm systems, and door locks. Unsurprisingly, it teams up with Google Assistant to create a connected home. Google Home Hub lets the owners see and control all compatible devices in a single dashboard so that homeowners can view visitors outside the door and family members in other rooms. The dashboard is not unlike that for building security guards, only "smarter".

GV (formerly Google Ventures): as the name suggests, GV provides capital for start-up companies in life science, healthcare, artificial intelligence, robotics, transportation, cyber security, and agriculture. Some of the invested companies were later acquired by Alphabet or became publicly-traded firms. Some of the invested companies that are better known to US consumers are: Uber (car-sharing company), Jet (a member-only online shopping site, which was later acquired by Walmart), and Blue Bottle (a coffee roaster, which was later acquired by Nestlé).[6]

CapitalG (formerly Google Capital): venture capital company, CapitalG, is a growth equity fund that invests in companies that "drive market disruption by harnessing long-term technology trends".[7] Companies that are invested in by Google also receive Google expertise in product, engineering, marketing, sales, and operations. Employees in these companies can also take lessons in machine learning offered by Alphabet. Better-known companies that offer consumer services are Lyft (car-sharing), Airbnb (home-sharing), Credit Karma (online credit-tracking), SurveyMonkey (online research software), and Glassdoor (online review of organizations).

Google Fiber: Internet service providers. At the time of writing, Google Fiber only serves a limited number of US cities. In some cities, they only serve apartments and condos.[8]

Chronicle: A cybersecurity company for organizations to manage and understand data.[9]

Alphabet's "Other bets" are said to be non-Internet-related businesses. But the Internet is a pre-existing condition under which some companies exist. For example, without the Internet, there would not be a need for Google Fiber or X, which both aim to provide Internet connection to users. Without the Internet, online sites of car-sharing and home-sharing services wouldn't exist. The "other" in "Other Bets" does not refer to *non*-Internet, but services where Google might find it hard to sell advertising space because some of the companies target business customers, others are start-up companies.

Even though Alphabet sets out to better humankind, the grand problems that it tries to solve only involve a handful of domains of human knowledge, such as life science, healthcare, artificial intelligence, robotics, transportation, cyber security, and agriculture. Alphabet believes that information is key to solving these problems, and also that all these problems can be solved through technology. For example, more healthcare information will help people make better decisions, and better artificial intelligence will understand how to analyze information. Alphabet does not set out to solve problems on the grand scale, for which solutions may or may not be related to information. For example, it does not seek to combat religious violence, sexism and racism, refugee crises, poverty, or hunger. Nor should it.

Alphabet is a profit-making business, not a governing body. However, the company, in particular X (the innovation lab), often uses a tone that is more appropriate for an international organization (such as the United Nations) and national governments to describe the work that it does. For example, X's Project Loon rationalized its importance by quoting the International Telecommunication Union (ITU), that one in two people in the world today has no Internet connection. Therefore, Alphabet charged itself to bring the Internet to remote places through stratospheric balloons. If Alphabet does not solve the problem, the consequence is said to be grave: "[half of the world's population] are completely left out of a digital revolution that could improve their finances, education, and health".[10] This tone is very similar to that of the ITU, which wrote "[we are] committed to connecting all the world's people—wherever they live and whatever their means. Through our work, we protect and support everyone's fundamental right to communicate".[11] By using a tone more suitable for an international organization, Alphabet implied that it filled in the gaps left by international organizations and national governments. For example, to show how X may actually provide services for disadvantaged populations, X wrote that the stratospheric balloons provided access to populations in Peru and Puerto Rico when natural disasters disconnected the regions from the Internet.[12] However, X's projects are not humanitarian in nature, the end goals are not to continuously provide for the disadvantaged or to level uneven technological development. X's technologies are developed for markets. When technologies mature, Alphabet will establish a new company to sell these technologies as commercial products and services.

Financial Data and Market Share

Is creating infinite time profitable? Apparently it is. Alphabet is one of the biggest corporations in the US, if not the world. According to *Forbes*, Alphabet is the eleventh largest company in the US.[13] Among corporations in the industries of telecommunications, information, and communication technologies, Alphabet is the fifth largest company, after Apple, AT&T, Verizon, and Microsoft. However, *Forbes* did not rank Alphabet as high as eleventh when it came to sales and assets. When compared to corporations that sell tangible goods such as consumer products and automobiles, Alphabet is only ranked at number 22 in sales. Alphabet is also ranked low in assets (at number 37); corporations with the most assets are all in financial services. However, information companies are all ranked high in market value. Alphabet is ranked as the second company with the largest market value, only coming behind Apple. Microsoft, Amazon, and Facebook are three other companies that are ranked in the top ten list of market value.

Alphabet is the 23rd largest company in the world.[14] Similar to the US ranking, Alphabet's global sales cannot compete with corporations that sell tangible goods and its assets cannot compete with investment banks and financial services. However, it has the third largest market value in the entire world. In addition to four other information technology giants based in the US (Apple, Microsoft, Amazon, Facebook), three other hi-tech companies are also ranked highly in market values: Alibaba and Tencent based in China, and Samsung based in South Korea.

Market value for a public company is also called market capitalization; it is calculated by the multiplication of the company's shares outstanding by the value of one share. The high market values of Alphabet and other information technologies show that the market is optimistic about the future stock performance of these companies. In other words, institutional investors such as banks and insurance companies believe that these companies represent the economy of the future. These companies are believed to experience greater growth even though their current sales are lower than those that sell tangible goods. On the other hand, "traditional" corporations, such as those in the automobile industry, have healthier sales than information technology companies but they are ranked with lower market values. This may mean that institutional investors believe that these companies have already passed their golden years and will not experience dramatic growth.

Growth is indeed a good word to describe how Google came into force from 2000 to 2013. I documented in Lee (2016) that from 2000 to 2013, revenue increased by 1,700 percent. Each year, the revenue grew by double, if not triple digits. Table 3.1 shows the revenues and net income of Google from 2013 to 2014 and Alphabet from 2015 to 2018.

Google continues to rely on the US as its largest market, with close to half its revenue coming from the domestic market. In 2017, 47 percent of its revenue came from the US; 32 percent came from Europe, the Middle East, and Africa; 14 percent came from Asia Pacific; and 5 percent from the other Americas (Alphabet, 2017).

Alphabet still recognizes that its main revenue came from online advertising. In 2017, 86 percent of Alphabet's revenue came from advertising (US $95,375 millions), but its revenue has been more diverse than in previous years. In 2015 and 2016, 90 percent and 88 percent of Alphabet's revenue came from advertising. Prior to 2012, before the company bought Motorola Mobility, more than 90 percent came from advertising. Other revenues were drawn from the sales of apps, in-app purchases, digital content products, and hardware, licensing, and service fees (Alphabet, 2017).

Table 3.1 Revenues and Net Income of Google and Alphabet, 2013–2017

	2013	2014	2015	2016	2017
Revenues (in millions)	55,519	66,001	74,989	90,272	110,855
Increase from the previous year (%)	12	19	14	20	23
Net income (loss) (in $1,000)	12,733	14,136	16,348	19,478	12,662

Source: Alphabet, 2017.

How Does Google Ads Make (So Much) Money?

Google believes that just as its search results provide relevant results, its online advertising services also provide relevant information to users. It sees ads as paid information. As such, they have to be labeled but relevant. Online advertising is seen to match the users with the advertisers. In Google's own words, "we show great ads for the right people" (Alphabet, 2015, p. 2). Google has two types of advertising plans: performance and brand.

Performance ads generate money by "pay by clicks": advertisers bid for keywords, but they only pay Google when users click on the ads. For example, when I searched with the keywords "good books on Google", the results first showed organic searches such as two fantasy books, one book translated from Portuguese, Steven Levy's *In the Plex* (2011), and "mommy porn" *Fifty Shades Darker.* Right underneath the organic searches were "sponsored" links (aka ads) that suggested three more titles and the vendors that sell them: the first one was an electronic book *The Beautiful Poetry of Donald Trump*, sold by Google Play, the second was the audio book *The Art of Thinking Clearly*, sold by Audible.com, and the third was *It's Not Supposed to be This Way*, sold by Target. If I clicked on any of the three sponsored links, the advertiser would pay Google for my click, which is called an "engagement". The trick for advertisers is that they have to guess the keywords users input to search for relevant products online. In this case, none of the three advertised books seemed to be relevant to my query of "good books on Google" so I did not click on any of the links. No money changed hands between Google and the advertisers Google Play, Audible, and Target.

Google has suggested that its online advertising system is democratic because both large and small merchants can do online bidding (Levy, 2011). This process is believed to disrupt the long-held tradition of ad buying. Traditionally, national brands such as Coca-Cola, Johnson & Johnson, and General Motors would mobilize a large amount of money to buy advertising *time* on television and radio as well as advertising *space* in print media. As a result, local manufacturers of sugary drinks and household products found it difficult to compete with companies endowed with large advertising budgets. Google's advertising program, AdSense, is then believed to have leveled the playing field. Local manufacturers can compete with national brands as long as their ads are relevant to users' searches. For example, a national brand that is willing to pay more money for a bid may not necessarily find their ads to be more prominently displayed than a local brand that pays less *if* the national brand's ads are deemed less relevant to the queries.

The second type of advertising is called brand advertising. The way it works is more like traditional advertising, yet Google claims that the primary purpose of these ads is not to sell products, but to raise users' awareness of and affinity with the brand. It also emphasizes branding across media and platforms: from videos, text, and images to interactive ads. Google makes money when the ads are shown on YouTube videos. YouTube users may notice that the ads shown before or during the video may not be relevant to the content of the video at all.

Competitors

Despite its size, Alphabet believes that it faces formidable competition from companies that offer "disruptive" technologies to the markets. As suggested, Google founders believed that new technological inventions could bring fast-moving, sweeping changes to societies. Inventions are seen to replace old technologies over night. Therefore, Alphabet believes that it needs to stay ahead in the competition in order to stay relevant.

In its 10K report, Alphabet lists (Alphabet, 2017) its major competitors in nine different markets:

(1) General search engines and information services: Baidu (based in China), Bing (owned by Microsoft), Naver (based in South Korea), Seznam (based in the Czech Republic), Yahoo! (owned by Verizon), and Yandex (based in Russia).

(2) Vertical search engines and e-commerce: examples given by Alphabet are Amazon and eBay, Kayak (travel services), and LinkedIn (professional networking). Alphabet sees these sites as competitors because users may search for products *directly* on these sites instead of going through Google Search.

(3) Social media: Facebook, Snapchat, and Twitter. Alphabet discontinued its social media site Google+ in 2018 and Orkut in 2014, but it still sees social media companies as competitors because users may receive information from these sites instead of a search engine.

(4) Online advertising and platforms: Amazon, AppNexus, Criteo, and Facebook.

(5) Other advertising: billboards, magazines, newspapers, radio, and television.

(6) Digital video services: Amazon, Facebook, Hulu (co-owned by NBCUniversal [which is owned by Comcast], Fox [which is owned by News Corp], and Disney), and Netflix.

(7) Consumer electronics: companies that design, manufacture, and market these products, including those that develop proprietary software.

(8) Enterprise cloud services: Alibaba, Amazon, and Microsoft.

(9) Digital assistant providers: Amazon, Apple, and Microsoft.

Alphabet acknowledges that they compete for both users and advertisers. However, it is important to distinguish users as actual consumers from users as human interactions. For tangible consumer products such as smartphones and smart home systems, Alphabet competes for actual consumers, because a user who already has an iPhone from Apple may not need a second phone from Google. However, for most Google services, Alphabet does not compete for *actual* individual consumers, but for the *time* that consumers spend on their services and the interaction they have with the algorithm. To Alphabet, there is no difference between a hundred consumers who conduct one search each and one consumer who does a hundred unique searches. Each unique search yields information about the users and each search results in sponsored links that can potentially be clicked on.

In other words, online services are unlike hardware because they are not exclusive: using services offered by Google's competitors does not *preclude* users from using Google's. For example, a user of Microsoft Office at work may still use Google Docs for other purposes. A user of Google Search for general purposes may use Amazon for specific purposes. Because Google users are not precluded from using services provided by Google's competitors, Alphabet needs to compete for users' time by infinitely expanding the time that they spend online: whether it is to increase the number of users to go online or to increase the time that users spend on Alphabet products and services. The many moonshot projects invested in by Alphabet are intended to increase the number of users that go online, especially among those who do not have reliable broadband Internet and mobile telephony. For the populations that are already online, the many new services that Alphabet offers increase the time that users spend online, whether it is through software installed in Google's hardware or "smart" home assistant.

Is There Real Competition?

To what extent is the competition suggested by Alphabet palpable? Even though Alphabet suggested that it competes with domestic and international companies in different markets, it actually only competes with four companies in the US: Amazon, Apple, Facebook, and Microsoft. In addition, even though these four companies compete in a number of markets (general and vertical search engines, social media, online advertising, digital video services, enterprise cloud services, and digital assistant providers), Alphabet dominates in a few markets while the three main competitors dominate others. The competition between the four companies is not as formidable as Alphabet has claimed. The market shares that Google has in seven markets show that the company leads in some but lags in others.

(1) Search engine: Google is still the dominant search engine on desktops/ laptops around the world, as of December 2018: it has 73.0 percent market share, while its named competitors Baidu has 13.3 percent, Bing (owned by Microsoft) has 7.9 percent, Yahoo! (owned by Verizon) has 3.7 percent, and Yandex has 1.1 percent. Its domination is more obvious on mobile phones and tablets on which 81.5 percent and 85.0 percent of respective searches were on Google Search.[15]

(2) Browser: Google's Chrome has 63.6 percent of market shares in the desktop/laptop browser market around the world as of December 2018. Microsoft's Internet Explorer has 11.2 percent and Apple's Safari has 3.8 percent. On mobile phones, Chrome has a similar market share but Apple's Safari has 26.7 percent. On tablets, Chrome and Safari both have about 45 percent. Safari's popularity on mobile phones and tablets is probably due to iPhone and iPad users using the built-in browser to a Google one, proving that linking hardware to software is an effective means to drive users to specific applications.[16]

(3) Enterprise cloud services: Amazon's web services have 41.5 percent market shares, Microsoft's Azure has 29.6 percent, and Alphabet's Google Cloud has 3.0 percent (Cole, 2018).

(4) Operating system: Microsoft's Windows is the dominant operating system around the world as of December 2018, accounting for 88 percent of the market. Apple's Mac OS accounted for 9.5 percent, and Alphabet's Chrome OS 0.3 percent. The domination of Windows is probably due to the fact that many personal computers are preloaded with Windows. Only the more sophisticated users would use Linux or Chrome OS. In the mobile phone market, Alphabet's Android has 70.1 percent of the market share and Apple's iOS has 28.5 percent.[17]

(5) Digital assistant provider: Amazon Alexa has 62 percent of the market share in 2017 while Alphabet's Google Assistant has 25 percent. However, it is predicted that Google Assistant will increase its market share to 43 percent in 2020 because of a lower price.[18]

(6) Smartphone: the smartphone market is slightly more competitive at the global level, probably due to a wider price range. The growing middle-class population in China may prefer the low price of the three home-grown brands (Huawei, Xiaomi, and Oppo) to that of US brands. From July to September 2018, Samsung (South Korea) has 20.3 percent of the global market share, Huawei (China) has 14.6 percent, Apple has 13.2 percent, Xiaomi (China) has 9.7 percent, and Oppo (China) has 8.4 percent. The rest, 33 percent of the market, is dominated by "others", including Alphabet's Pixel.[19] In the US, during the same time period, Apple led the market with 39 percent market share, Samsung 25 percent, LG (South Korea) 17 percent, Motorola (owned by Levono, based

in Hong Kong) 8 percent, and others 11 percent. The domestic smart-phone market is less competitive. (Google once owned Motorola from 2012 to 2014, but then it was sold to Hong Kong-based Lenovo).

(7) Tablet: from April to June 2018, Apple had 35 percent of the market share worldwide while Samsung had 16 percent (Vanian, 2018). Amazon only had 4.4 percent of the market as of 2017 (Dignan, 2017).

(8) Laptop: HP led the global market with 24.3 percent in the global laptop market in 2016, Lenovo 4.9 percent, Dell 15.2 percent, and Apple 9.6 percent (Indo-Asian News Service, 2018).

The four companies Alphabet, Microsoft, Amazon, and Apple compete in a number of markets but Google still dominates the search market on all platforms as well as on the browser and operating systems for mobile devices. With the expected growth of mobile devices worldwide, Alphabet will probably see growth in the markets of search, browser, and operating systems. Alphabet, however, accounts for an insignificant market share in consumer hardware such as smartphone, tablet, and laptop. Microsoft still maintains its domination in the desktop operating system but lags behind in search, browser, and cloud services. However, since Microsoft is still the default choice for many workplaces, Alphabet is less likely to challenge its domination in the desktop market. Apple dominates the hardware market and is the only US company that has a significant global market share in the smartphone, tablet, and laptop sector. However, the hardware market seems to be more competitive worldwide because China-based competitors can make cheaper hardware. It is unknown if Alphabet can compete in this area domestically and globally at all. Amazon dominates the markets of cloud services and digital assistant services, however, Alphabet is gaining a sizable market share in these areas and is expected to dominate the digital assistant services market.

The analysis of these various markets does not show that Alphabet is in formidable competition because too few companies are competing. All the competitors hold a leading edge in one or more markets. The markets for hardware are slightly more competitive, probably because the cost for making hardware can be driven down by cheaper labor. In software markets such as search engines, operating systems, and cloud services, US-based companies dominate the global markets, possibly due to the significant amount of research and development resources required. In addition, the US government teams up with corporations to try to ensure that intellectual property remains in private hands.

Typical Strategies

In Lee (2016), I identified two strategies that Google used to increase market share and amass innovative products: a huge research and development

(R&D) budget and acquisition of start-up companies. Alphabet justified a huge budget in R&D because of its vulnerable position in various markets: "our businesses are rapidly evolving, intensely competitive, and subject to changing technologies"; "competing successfully depends heavily on our ability to accurately anticipate developments and deliver innovative, relevant and useful products, services, and technologies to the marketplace in a timely manner"; "the competitive pressure to innovate will encompass a wider range of products and services, including [those] that may be outside of our historical core business" (Alphabet, 2017, p. 7). The vulnerable position expressed by Alphabet is not supported by my analysis of Alphabet's competition in various markets: even though it does not lead in every market in which it has businesses, there are not many companies competing in most of these markets. The sense of vulnerability reinforces the belief in disruptive technology and creative destruction. It also gives a sense that the company is always about "newness" (see Chapter 5, "Cultural Profile"). Alphabet invested in R&D in the areas of advertising, cloud, machine learning, search, and new products and services. It had more employees in R&D than in sales and marketing. In 2016, about 36 percent of its employees worked in R&D.[20] The number of employees matches with R&D spending. From 2008 to 2017, Alphabet increased the budget five fold, from US$2.8 billion to US$16.6 billion.

Another strategy that Alphabet uses to increase market shares is to acquire start-up companies. Some of the earlier acquisitions became key services provided by Google. For example, in 2004 Google acquired Keyhole, which became Google Earth. In 2005, it acquired the Android mobile phone operating system. In 2006, Google acquired YouTube, which became the second most-visited site in the world. It also acquired backend technologies to improve its online advertising system such as DoubleClick in 2007 and AdMob in 2010.

Since the launching of Alphabet in October 2015, it has acquired 41 companies whose names are unfamiliar to the average consumer. These companies are in the areas of mobile software, consumer electronics, scientific and engineering, Internet software, artificial intelligence, healthcare, development tools, cloud platform, media and entertainment, search, and commerce.[21] As shown earlier, Capital G and GV (venture capitalist firms) under Alphabet also invested in start-ups, which were later acquired by the company.

Conclusion

The growth of Alphabet relies on a network of capital. Capital here does not only refer to money or labor-power, but the infinite time and multiple spaces that the Internet seems to create. As a search engine, Google indexes a large number of sites and promises users that it answers queries with the most relevant information. Being the most visited site around the world, Google. com attracts a large number of users. According to Ardor Seo, Google.com handled 63,000 searches per second in 2018.[22] The large number of users means a large number of search results and accompanying advertisements are shown each second. The large number of advertisements shown makes the search engine appear to have created many spaces for ads to be shown and viewed. As a result, the network appears to have effectively overcome the time and space constraints of capitalism.

The infinite time that the Internet seems to have created fuels the fast growth of Alphabet. The company's revenue has experienced staggering growth since Google went public. The company has experienced double-digit growth in revenue every year. The only year it slowed down was during the 2008 recession. However, it still came out of it unharmed, as evidenced by the high market valuation rated by investors. Together with Alphabet, three other US-based hi-tech companies (Amazon, Apple, and Microsoft) are also believed to continue to grow and lead the world economy. In contrast, big companies in retail and the automobile industry are assumed to have saturated markets. Despite Google's unshaken domination in the hi-tech industry, it tries to paint itself as being in a vulnerable position. The very reason why Alphabet was formed is because of the assumed destructive nature of new technologies: if Alphabet fails to be ahead of the game, it will become obsolete. However, an analysis of the markets in which Alphabet competes shows that competition hardly exists because there are so few competitors. If Alphabet should get absorbed by another company, it will probably be by one of its peers rather than a start-up company.

I explained that the formation of Alphabet came from the desire to create infinite time: even if time seems to be infinite and spaces seem to be multiple, there are always a finite number of world populations. At present, Alphabet's solution is to exhaust unconnected populations by providing the Internet to remote areas. It also tries to increase the number of Android operating system users by selling hardware. In addition, Alphabet diversifies its businesses by moving toward information-based biotechnology and self-driving cars. At present, it is unknown if these new ventures will help the corporation grow or if they will remain special projects that do not translate into real profits. Whether Alphabet will be successful at diversifying its business or not, it is more than a collection of different companies. It is a conglomerate.

Notes

1 The Office of Technology Licensing (OTL). Stanford University. https://otl.stanford.edu/ Accessed: 26th December, 2018.
2 The top 500 sites on the web. Alexa. www.alexa.com/topsites. Accessed: 21st December, 2018.

3   The Moonshot Factory. X. https://x.company/. Accessed: 21st December, 2018.
4   Verily Projects. Verily. https://verily.com/. Last accessed: 21st December, 2018.
5   Calico. www.calicolabs.com/. Accessed: 21st December, 2018.
6   Portfolio. GV. www.gv.com/. Accessed: 21st December, 2018.
7   Growth stage investing. CapitalG. https://capitalg.com/. Accessed: 21st December, 2018.
8   Fiber cities. Google Fiber. https://fiber.google.com/about/. Accessed: 21st December, 2018.
9   Approach. Chronicle. https://chronicle.security/technology/. Accessed: 21st December, 2018.
10 Loon. X. https://x.company/projects/loon/. Accessed: 21st December, 2018.
11 About International Telecommunication Union (ITU). ITU. www.itu.int/en/about/Pages/default.aspx. Accessed: 21st December, 2018.
12 See endnote 9.
13 Alphabet. Forbes. www.forbes.com/companies/alphabet/?list=top-public-companies#593d3733540e. Accessed: 21st December, 2018.
14 The world's largest public companies. Forbes. www.forbes.com/global2000/list/#header:marketValue_sortreverse:true. Accessed: 21st December, 2018.
15 Net Marketshare. https://netmarketshare.com/. Accessed: 22nd December, 2018.
16 See endnote 14.
17 See endnote 14.
18 Worldwide intelligent/digital assistant market share in 2017 and 2020, by product. Statista.com. www.statista.com/statistics/789633/worldwide-digital-assistant-market-share/. Accessed: 22nd December, 2018.
19 Global market share held by leading smartphone vendors from 4th quarter 2009 to 3rd quarter 2018. Statista.com. www.statista.com/statistics/271496/global-market-share-held-by-smartphone-vendors-since-4th-quarter-2009/ Accessed: 22nd December, 2018.
20 Number of full-time Alphabet employees from 2008 to 2016, by department. Statista.com. www.statista.com/statistics/219333/number-of-google-employees-by-department/ Accessed: 23rd December, 2018.
21 The Google acquisition tracker. CBInsights.com. www.cbinsights.com/research-google-acquisitions. Accessed: 23rd December, 2018.
22 "How many Google searches per day on average in 2018?" Ardor Seo. https://ardorseo.com/blog/how-many-google-searches-per-day-2018/ Accessed: 29th December, 2018.

Bibliography

Alphabet. (2015). *Alphabet Inc. and Google Inc. Form 10-K*. Mountain View, CA: Alphabet. Retrieved from: https://abc.xyz/investor/static/pdf/20151231_alphabet_10K.pdf?cache=5400095. Last accessed: 17th December, 2018.

Alphabet. (2017). *Alphabet Inc. and Google Inc. Form 10-K*. Mountain View, CA: Alphabet. Retrieved from: www.sec.gov/Archives/edgar/data/1652044/000165204418000007/goog10-kq42017.htm#s14f5a997f3dc460a88541e628f42630b. Accessed: 18th December, 2018.

Cole, C. (2018, July 30). Cloud market in 2018 and predictions for 2021. *Skyhighnetworks.com*. Retrieved from: www.skyhighnetworks.com/cloud-secur

ity-blog/microsoft-azure-closes-iaas-adoption-gap-with-amazon-aws/. Accessed: 22nd December, 2018.

Dignan, L. (2017, November 3). Amazon gains share in declining tablet market, Apple's iPad still No. 1. *ZDNet*. Retrieved from: www.zdnet.com/article/amazon-gains-share-in-declining-tablet-market-apples-ipad-still-no-1/. Accessed: 22nd December, 2018.

Gallagher, D. (2018, January 10). Why the U.S. smartphone market is hard to crack. *Wall Street Journal*. Retrieved from: www.wsj.com/articles/why-the-u-s-smartph one-market-is-hard-to-crack-1515583800. Accessed: 20th December, 2018.

Indo-Asian News Service. (2018). HP leads global laptop market, Apple takes fourth place: Trendforce. *Gadgets360*. Retrieved from: https://gadgets.ndtv.com/laptops/ news/hp-leads-global-laptop-market-apple-takes-fourth-place-trendforce-1812063. Accessed: 22nd December, 2018.

International Telecommunication Union. (2018). *Measuring the information society report: Executive summary 2018*. Geneva, Switzerland: ITU.

Lee, M. (2010). *Free information? The case against Google*. Champaign, IL: Common Ground.

Lee, M. (2011). Google ads and the blindspot debate. *Media, Culture, and Society*, *33*(3), 433–448.

Lee, M. (2016). Google: Information organizer. In: B. J. Birkinbine, R. Gomez, & J. Wasko (Eds.), *Global media giants* (pp. 398–412). New York: Routledge.

Levy, S. (2011). *In the plex: How Google thinks, works, and shapes our lives*. New York: Simon & Schuster.

Marx, K. (1867/1887). *Capital Volume I*. Retrieved from: www.marxists.org/archive/ marx/works/download/pdf/Capital-Volume-I.pdf. Accessed: 2nd April, 2019.

Page, L. (2015). G is for Google. *Alphabet*. Retrieved from: https://abc.xyz/. Accessed: 17th December, 2018.

Vanian, J. (2018, August 2). Tablet sales are on the decline, but Apple and Samsung are leaving Amazon in the dust. *Fortune*. Retrieved from: http://fortune.com/ 2018/08/02/apple-samsung-tablet-market/. Accessed: 22nd December, 2018.

4 Political Profile

How power is created and dispersed in a network is the central question of this chapter. Power is an enduring issue in a political economy of communication. Political economists usually see power as negative because they associate it with concepts such as domination and subordination, control, and surveillance. Political economists tend to think power resides with only individuals and organizations, although some have begun to explore how it resides with algorithms (Bilić, 2018). Therefore, an ANT approach may challenge a political-economic conceptualization of power by pointing out that people and organizations are *only* powerful when they are associated in networks. People and organizations on their own cannot be powerful. The more connections individuals and organizations have in a network, the more powerful they are (Latour, 2005). Networks not only make individuals and organizations powerful, but they also give individuals and organizations visibility when their names are included on websites generated in search results. Individuals with less power have fewer connections in networks, which in turn render them invisible. In this chapter, we consider how power is generated and distributed in three types of networks (ownership of corporations, boards of directors, and lobbying). Network visualization illustrates how powerful individuals and organizations connect with each other. In the following, I first discuss how a political economy of communication conceptualizes power, then I discuss how Actor-Network Theory (ANT) sees it. I conclude by suggesting how this chapter conceptualizes the concept.

Power in a Political Economy of Communication

In this section, I consider how political economists in the field of communication conceptualize power, in particular how power is produced and circulated in a digital economy. Mosco (2009) suggested that political economists want to find out how social relations, in particular, power relations, "mutually constitute the production, distribution, and consumption of resources, including communication resources" (Mosco, 2009, p. 2). He later argued in *The Digital Sublime* (2004) that while concepts such as commodification, spatialization, and structuration are useful in order to understand how power works in media and information sectors, political-economic concepts alone cannot explain why power sustains in a digital economy. He, therefore, proposed that a cultural understanding of the digital economy would enhance a political-economic critique. Borrowing Barthes' concept of myth (2012), Mosco argued that the digital economy is a myth, an ahistorical truth. The process of myth-making can be revealed by showing how myth and power mutually constitute each other. Mosco sees power from a negative light because it addresses why some populations get more resources at the expense of others and why those who have fewer resources are willing to keep on being exploited.

Another political economist who believes that power is negative is McChesney (2014). He highlighted that large corporations are sources of power. In highly concentrated industries such as media and telecommunications, corporations gain power through ownership. When a handful of corporations own the majority of the markets in both "new" and "old" media, they have the power to decide who can enter the markets and what will be produced for the consumers. Consequently, a concentrated media industry harms democracy because it reduces competition and endangers a marketplace of ideas. He believed that a political economic approach would shed light on an alternative arrangement of the media economy.

Winseck (2016) disagreed with McChesney (2014) about the power held by media corporations. He believed the mobile wireless and Internet-centric communication system is much more powerful than a concentrated media. He also pointed out that corporations are not the only source of power, governments often co-operate with corporations to exercise power over users.

Yet another political economist believed that power works in a dynamic way in the media. Fuchs (2011) believed that the media are "fields for the display of power, counter-power, domination and sites of power struggles" (p. 5). He gave the example that while Facebook is a corporation that has power over its users, users nonetheless can use it for online protests. However, even though the media can be sites of power struggle, power is also seen as negative because Fuchs believes that asymmetrical power relations enable domination from one group to others.

The earlier discussion shows that political economists tend to agree with what power is and how it shapes social relations. I argue that one blind spot concerning these views of power is that they seem to agree that *power can only reside with human beings and organizations*. For example, media owners have more power than media users, big media corporations have more power than alternative media. Power is then like a possession, a "thing" that can be owned and exercised on others. Less powerful players who challenge unequal social relations are supposed to ask for the power to be shared.

Political economists are not alone in believing that power resides with people and corporations. In the critique of Google, scholars with a critical perspective very often pointed out the immense power that Google—the corporation, the technology, the owners—has over political and social lives. For example, Segev (2010) and Jeanneney (2007) believed that Google maintains a domination of the English language in the organization of knowledge: the search engine overlooks non-English websites. Vaidhyanathan (2011) wrote that Google is amassing information for private gain but is often mistaken as a public goods provider. He questioned what will happen to those privately-owned data when the company ceases to exist. Noble (2018) suggested that the Google way of organizing information reinforces a White-dominated worldview in which people of color are marginalized, sexualized, and commodified. She believed that Google employees are directly exercising power over users by influencing their views on race.

When Google technologies are being critiqued, scholars tend to suggest that code developers and engineers are the ones who are *directly* responsible for the bias in technologies. Noble (2018) asked pointedly, "if Google software engineers are not responsible for the design of their algorithms, then who is?" (p. 66). This question is similar to one that political economists would ask: if powerful players such as media owners, executives, and politicians are not responsible for a concentrated media, then who is? From this perspective, when organizations are owned and managed by powerful individuals, the organizations are assumed to be automatically powerful entities. Moreover, powerful individuals and organizations are believed to exert domination over others such as workers, unsuspecting consumers, minority groups, non-English-speaking populations, and smaller companies. The dominated groups, being left with few choices in an unequal relation, can either choose to submit to the control or band together to revolt. By seeing humans as the only agency to exercise power, the aforementioned scholars did not consider whether power might be originated from technologies (hardware, software, discourses, formulae, algorithms) when humans associate with them in the network. By taking into account the relationships between humans and non-humans in a network, I argue how political economists and critical scholars can problematize the notion of power in a more fruitful way.

Actor-Network Theory and Power

I argue in this section that ANT could provide political economists with a conceptualization of power that takes into account how power is created and distributed in networks of humans and non-humans. ANT does not assume that humans are the only actors with agency in a network. Also, ANT does not believe that humans are superior to non-humans (Callon & Law, 1995).

Metaphorically, power is not seen as a "thing" that individuals and organizations collect and store in a vault, but it is created, circulated, and renewed in networks made up of individuals and "things" (such as technologies, written documents, infrastructure, buildings). To give an example, the founders of Google, Sergey Brin and Larry Page, are often called powerful individuals. Some may explain their power in terms of their wealth, intellect, political clout, and technological knowledge. However, if we imagine a hypothetical scenario in which both of them are stranded on a desert island with no resources, they may be as powerful (or powerless) as most able-bodied adults. In this desert island scenario, the networks to which Brin and Page belong are cut off. Even if both of them carry stacks of cash, money has nowhere to circulate. Even if both of them have many powerful friends and acquaintances, no one can be reached. Even if both of them have mastery of computing, no material is available to construct a computer.

Some will undoubtedly suggest that as long as Brin and Page carry a charged computing device, they may have a chance to connect to Wifi to seek help. After all, X (an Alphabet's business) launched the Loon Balloon project to bring Internet access in the remote parts of the world.[1] In this real-life scenario, Brin and Page still have more power than an average able-bodied adult because their private jets will be immediately deployed to rescue them. This is correct, but the point of the desert island scenario is that the circulation of power completely relies on the network of humans and "things": computing devices, Wi-Fi networks, and private jets. Without them, networks do not exist.

Incorporating the concept of power in human–non-human networks is however a task with very little fanfare from both ANT and political economy. ANT scholars do not believe that a macrostructure exists (Callon, 2007), therefore there is no such thing called capitalism. They believe in the specificities of different markets because each of them is made up of different humans and non-humans. Because markets are heterogeneous, a single concept such as power is not enough to explain how all the markets work. Some political economists (such as Fine, 2005; Gareau, 2005) countered ANT by suggesting that it has ignored the homogenizing power of capitalist markets. Capitalism is believed to be such a powerful force that it homogenizes all variants in the network. Therefore, Fine (2005) called for a critical political economy to understand the historical nature of capital and to examine the dialectics of the unfolding of structures, processes, relations, and tendencies.

Some political economists believe that a successful incorporation of ANT into the political economy is only possible when a "weaker" version of ANT is used. A weaker version of ANT can keep its belief in non-human's agency but needs to acknowledge that actor-networks are driven by similar global and systematic processes, social processes are more directive than natural, and power is asymmetrical. Media studies scholars such as Couldry (2005) also believe that a successful incorporation of ANT and political economy requires an acknowledgment that there are power differentials between human and non-human actors. Human actors are argued to matter more because "social consequences that are linked to how these differences are interpreted and how they affect the various agents' ability to have their interpretations of the world stick" (p. 102).

This chapter acknowledges that there may be power differentials between human and non-human actors because computing networks are after all designed by humans. Humans are the only species who can articulate how to act on the material world so that materials can be made useful to social lives. However, this chapter also acknowledges that human–non-human networks enable humans to do things that are otherwise impossible. The desert island scenario shows that natural resources need to be extracted and engineered for the survival of human beings. In the absence of non-humans (raw materials, tools), humans may not easily form networks that enable their survival.

How This Chapter Conceptualizes Power

Power is produced and circulated in networks. However, I refuse to see networks as purely online or offline, solely humans or machines. I see networks connect humans and machines in the material world: whether human relationships are built through online or in personal communication, whether technologies enable humans to communicate through the Internet or in person. In this definition, few human beings are excluded from any network. Even among the illiterates, the elderly, and the technology abstainer, once they communicate with other human beings and non-human objects in the material world, they are in a network. The production and circulation of power rely on a material space where communication takes place. For example, a conversation between parents and children in the kitchen may produce power that governs how the household is run, but this power has much less consequence on other families and societies. However, a conversation in the corporation's boardroom will have an impact on employees, their families, and other corporations. The power generated in a boardroom does not originate from the board members but the connections that they have with others outside the boardroom as well as technical objects that bind members together. Board members are usually notable members of their own organizations and communities. They are selected because of the perceived useful connections that they bring to the organizations. In contrast, parents do not select their children because of their perceived connection; children can definitely not select parents.

Similarly, technical objects such as bylaws of the board, employee contracts, and an organization's mission act on human actors as well. For example, bylaws and regulations exert power on board members; and employment contracts tell workers the organization's expectation of their job duties and performance. In this sense, bylaws and contracts are more than pieces of papers, they regulate human behavior and thoughts. In Foucault's conceptualization of power (1971), bylaws and contracts constitute a discourse that creates subjects such as board members and employees. In this discourse, board members are asked to act and behave like board members, to think of how an organization benefits because of them. Similarly, employees are conscious of what they are expected to do and not because of the contracts. In the following three networks, I included both human and non-human actors (lobbying bills, organizations) to understand how power is circulated.

A Network of Google Ownership

Google became a public company when it held its initial public offering (IPO) in 2004, and has been traded on Nasdaq as GOOGL. Public companies such as Google are conceptualized as a contractual nexus driven by signals on financial markets (Davis, 2009). How do the concepts of network and power explain why Google went public? What is Nasdaq? Where is it located? Who owns Alphabet?

Why Did Google Go Public?

It may appear to be natural that any tech start-ups *should* become a public company or be acquired by a bigger company. As shown in Chapter 3, "Economic Profile", the two venture capital firms under Alphabet invested in companies that have become public companies or have been acquired. The venture capital businesses of Alphabet follow the model of the Silicon Valley funding model: first, technology inventors secure funds from angel investors and venture capitalists. Then venture capitalists work with investment banks hoping the companies will go public. In the latter case, being acquired by a bigger company helps a start-up to tap into more resources. As I showed in Chapter 2, "History", Google documentarians rarely questioned why raising money through the stock market or being acquired by a larger corporation is required for tech start-ups. By not asking why firms need to raise funds or seek acquisition, online knowledge about Google implies that growth is the most important, if not the only, goal in capitalism. When growth becomes the *only* goal, then tech start-up firms may be assessed to have higher values than their actual worth. The dot-com craze and subsequent financial collapse in the 1990s exemplified one result of the obsession with growth.

While growth is seen as the only virtue in capitalism, few would like to remember that some tech darlings in the 1990s did not grow bigger, and some even became obsolete. For example, Netscape and Lyco that made IPOs in 1995 and 1996, respectively, became rudimentary web portals. The once dominant web portal Yahoo! was acquired by Verizon. The popularity of Yahoo! search and e-mail services has dwindled since Google Search and GMail entered the market. Despite past lessons, today's social media darlings, such as LinkedIn, Facebook, and Snapchat are perceived to be able to withstand economic stagnation and are believed to be able to grow indefinitely. When a tech mammoth does not grow as fast as expected, it will make the headlines of business newspapers such as *The Wall Street Journal*. For example, when Apple fell short of its projections for iPhone sales in early 2019, *The Wall Street Journal* ran a front-page story that implied an economic slowdown in China may lead to a slowdown in the global economy. As a public company, Alphabet will not grow indefinitely. It will become obsolete one day.

What and Where is Nasdaq?

Just as going public appears to be natural for tech start-ups, Nasdaq also appears to be the default stock exchange for technology companies. The scene on the day when Google went public was later replayed by many other tech companies such as Dropbox, Facebook, and Etsy. On the first day when Google was publicly traded on Nasdaq, cofounder Larry Page and CEO Eric Schmidt were photographed at Nasdaq celebrating the occasion. Projected on the back of the stage was Google's colorful logo, and erected before the crowd of executives was a podium with the Nasdaq logo.

Nasdaq appears to be a natural exchange for information tech companies. Six hundred and thirty technology companies are listed on Nasdaq, including some of the largest information technology companies such as Apple, Microsoft, Facebook, Intel, Cisco, Oracle, Adobe, and IBM. In contrast, only 173 technology companies are listed on the New York Stock Exchange (NYSE) and they tend to be companies that the consumers are unfamiliar with, such as Taiwan Semiconductor, SAP, and Illinois Tool Works. How stocks trade on Nasdaq and NYSE may explain tech companies' preference for the former.

Stock exchanges are networks: whether trading is done in person or through the computers. The New York Stock Exchange, being the oldest exchange in the country, has always been seen as the most prestigious exchange. Historically, traders have to pay a hefty sum to buy a seat in the exchange (Gordon, 1999). Companies that wish to be listed on the NYSE must have a minimum of $40 million in the value of publicly held shares,[2] however, Nasdaq only asks for $1 million. Nasdaq was launched as an alternative to NYSE in 1971. It was set up to tap into the scattered and disconnected penny stock markets that had a low entry barrier for traders. Nasdaq then served as a natural home for information technology companies that were once seen as fringe companies, not financially viable enough to be listed in NYSE.

Another explanation of why Nasdaq may hold more appeal for tech companies is that it has always been a computer network. Unlike NYSE that has a trading floor on which traders form a person-to-person network both inside "the pit" and with their clients, Nasdaq traders do business over the computer and the phone (Lee, 2014). Human–computer interaction on Nasdaq is not unlike that of online searches, because the computer-based networks enable human interaction, which produces information. In the case of Nasdaq, traders buy and sell through the computer and the phone. Price updates on the screen in turn prompt the traders to act on the information they see there: to buy, to sell, or not to act. A similar human–computer interaction takes place with Google Search: a query yields information that prompts the users to act. As suggested at the end of Chapter 2, "History", the Google Search algorithm and content producers form an intersubjective relationship: because of the way Google Search ranks websites, content producers learn how search engine optimization works.

In both the cases of Nasdaq and Google Search, the networks are constantly renewing themselves because of the quick flow of information. The networks may, however, experience an abruptly quick reconfiguration if a large number of human and/or non-human actors coordinate their activities. For example, in a market panic, traders slow down the buying and selling of stocks, which leads to a slowdown of activities in the network, resulting in a reduction in market liquidity. This phenomenon is more commonly called a financial crisis. Similarly, concerted activities online will produce a search crisis: when a large number of websites link to a specific webpage using specific words in the hyperlink, it can lead to a Google bomb. To make a Google bomb successful, content providers (such as bloggers) usually respond to a call to collectively take action so that they can manipulate a search result. For example, during the presidential election season in 2004, a search with the keywords "miserable failure" came back with the official White House page of President George W. Bush.

Who Owns a Public Company?

Political economists are keen to find out who owns a public company. While the public may associate well-known tech companies with the founders (such as Bill Gates and Microsoft, Jeff Bezos and Amazon), people may not know these companies are owned by institutional shareholders as well. According to *Forbes* (Stoller, 2018), 130 out of 2,000 largest global corporations are tech companies. The largest ten are household names not only in the US but also around the globe: Apple, Samsung, Microsoft, Alphabet, Intel, IBM, Facebook, Tencent, Hon Hai Precision, and Oracle. Some large companies are, however, privately owned. For example, Bloomberg, a financial information company, is owned by the Bloomberg family and its stocks are not available to the public.

When a company does an IPO, it usually issues shares to the founders, investors, and early employees. These people become individual shareholders. Late-coming executives may also become individual shareholders at a later date. The rest of the shares will be offered to the public through the stock markets. Although a stock offering to the public may appear to be a "democratic" way to share wealth with the population, the initial stock prices of companies such as Google and Spotify are often so exorbitantly high that they prohibit most people from owning the stock. Therefore, public companies such as mutual funds companies, investment banks, and insurance companies become institutional shareholders of these high-valued companies.

Mutual fund companies generate funds through individuals' retirement plans and insurance schemes. On the surface, these plans appear to allow individuals to share the wealth of the stock markets, but they are also structured to reduce risks for employers and governments and place them, instead, on employees and citizens (Davis, 2009). Mutual funds became popular among the employed when employers ceased to offer retirement benefits such as pension funds and when governments scaled down old-age protection for citizens. By investing their income in mutual funds, the working population is asked to take up risks by investing their income in the stock markets. Because of this, the stock performance of tech companies became relevant to the working population. Their retirement money depends on stock market performance, which in turn depends on well-performing hi-tech stocks. A well-performing stock market seems to make *everyone* gain. In this sense, mutual funds are perceived as networks made up of millions, if not billions, of individual customers. The networks are believed to distribute wealth because a large number of individuals pull their resources together to own stocks that are prohibitively expensive for an average worker. However, a network analysis (see Figure 4.1) will show that the major actors who determine stock values are actually some of the largest corporations. In the network of Alphabet's ownership, individual customers are invisible.

Figure 4.1 shows how power circulates in the stock markets through the ownership of Alphabet stocks. The figure shows the network of Alphabet's institutional owners as of June 30th, 2018. Information on the largest individual and institutional owners of public companies traded on Nasdaq can be found on Nasdaq.com. Google stocks had 2,282 holders, who collectively owned 240 million shares. Each share was valued at approximately $1,000 as

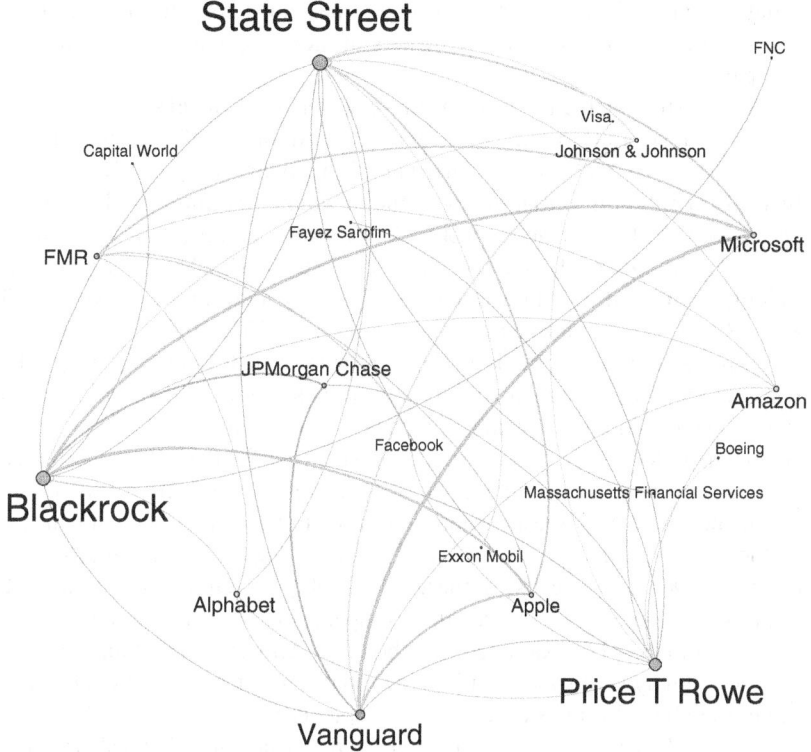

Figure 4.1 Ownership of Alphabet.

of late 2018, making the total shares worth US $240 billion. The stock value is staggering given the GDPs of Vietnam, Romania, and Portugal are each around US $240 billion. More shocking is that the GDPs of a few countries (Bhutan, Central African Republic, and Djibouti) are only one percent of the worth of Alphabet stocks.[3]

Close to 70 percent of Alphabet stocks were owned by institutions—the top five are Vanguard, Blackrock, State Street, FMR, and T. Price Rowe. All of them are investment banks and financial services companies. These five financial companies together own 73 million shares of Alphabet stocks that were valued at US $73 billion in late 2018. These five financial companies also own a large number of stocks in other companies. Some are in technology (Apple, Microsoft, Amazon, Facebook), others are in financial services (JPMorgan Chase, Visa), consumer products (Johnson & Johnson), energy (Exxon Mobil), and transport (Boeing). Even though brand names such as Apple and Amazon are more familiar to the average consumers than

Vanguard and Blackrock, the consumers may not know that financial services companies are actually the owners of these popular consumer product companies.

The question is, then, who owns these powerful financial services companies? The answer is that they own each other! Among the five largest institutional owners of Alphabet, Vanguard and Fidelity are not publicly traded, so there is no public information about them. Among the three publicly traded companies (T. Rowe Price, Blackrock, and State Street), T. Rowe Price is owned by Vanguard, Blackrock, and State Street; Blackrock is owned by Fidelity, Vanguard, Blackrock, and State Street; State Street is owned by T. Price Rowe, Vanguard, Blackrock, and State Street! This incestuous relationship implies that while stock markets are said to distribute risks by pulling resources together, they actually do not, because some of the largest corporations own each other. Once a company in the network has an unexpected financial performance, it will affect the stock performance of institutional owners. This incestuous relationship is, however, very effective at maintaining the power of the largest corporations, not only because of how much each of them owns, *but also because of the relationships that they establish by owning each other*. Because of these relationships, the most important stakeholders of these companies are other companies in the network, not customers or employees. For example, if the board of Alphabet makes an important decision, it may well first consider how it will impact its institutional owners rather than how it affects customers or employees.

Figure 4.1 shows how power circulates in the ownership of Alphabet. Names in the larger font styles are more powerful because they own the largest number of shares of other companies. State Street, Blackrock, and T. Price Rowe are three companies that own the most of the other companies in terms of the number of stocks. (I opted to use number of stocks, not the value of stocks due to price fluctuations). In turn, brand names that are familiar to consumers such as Alphabet, Amazon, and Apple are less powerful in the network because their shares are owned by the more powerful companies. The thickness of the lines indicates the strength of relationships: the thicker the line is, the more shares a financial service company owns of other companies. For example, Vanguard has a stronger relationship with Microsoft, Apple, and JPMorgan Chase than with Alphabet. Blackrock also has a stronger relationship with Microsoft, Apple, JPMorgan Chase than with Alphabet.

Board of Directors

I have shown in an earlier section that even though Google is a powerful company, its decisions are constrained by the major institutional shareholders. In this section, I show that even though the founders Sergey Brin and Larry

Page are seen as powerful individuals, their decisions are also constrained by the other individuals who make up the board of directors.

Both public and private companies may have boards of directors that oversee the executive board. The board of directors makes decisions such as the hiring and firing of executives, giving compensation (salary, stocks, allowances) to executives, approving company mission and vision, and ensuring that the company achieves its goals. In principle, the board keeps the power of the CEO, president, and executives in check. However, the actual workings of the board depend on the relationship between the board members and the executive boards. In some cases, executives also serve on the board. The dual roles sometimes create a conflict of interest, as shown in the case of Elon Musk, who was once both the CEO and the board chairperson of Tesla, an electric car company. In 2018, Tesla was investigated by the US Securities and Exchange Commission and the Department of Justice about its production performance and disclosure of insider trade information. Musk stepped down as the board chairperson in order to regain confidence from the public and the regulatory bodies.

Alphabet, like any public company, needs to disclose its board of directors to investors. As of 2018, Alphabet's board has 11 directors. I will first list who they are before diving into their relationships with other individuals and organizations.

Board members are usually nominated by other board members and are notable members in the public and private sectors. Some are CEOs of other corporations, some are university presidents and prominent faculty members, some work in public services. Because the board is charged with safeguarding the organization, they are drawn from the organization itself or closely-related industries. Among the 11 board members of Alphabet, 6 are Google insiders: they are the founders and executives of Google. Some are early investors, such as L. John Doerr whose company Kleiner Perkins invested in Google before it was incorporated. Except for two members (Roger W. Ferguson and Alan R. Mulally), all board members are Silicon Valley insiders, they have owned and worked for companies in the hi-tech industry.

Because the board members are executives and investors of Alphabet as well as other hi-tech companies, decision-making reinforces the domination of the industry in the US and abroad, as well as the domination of executives over managers and workers. Because of their professions and experiences, the board members tend not to question why the hi-tech industry is so prominent in the US economy. They may also not ask the company to expand to industries that are deemed lo-tech, such as textile manufacturing or small-scale farming. Similarly, because the value of their assets depends, at least partly, on the value of Alphabet stocks, they will not make decisions that directly harm the company's financial health, such as profit-sharing with every employee, encouraging workers to form unions, or reducing the compensation of top executives.

Where does the power of the board come from? How can 11 people make decisions for 10,000 employees and billions of users? From an Actor-Network Theory perspective, what gives the board power is the bylaws. The 22-page bylaws document for Alphabet[4] states how board members will be nominated, how often meetings occur, how voting is to be carried out, and what committees members can sit on. By agreeing to serve on the board, members are asked to abide by the bylaws. In the network of the board of directors, the bylaws are the instruments that bind the human actors together. Without the bylaws, the human actors do not have the power to make decisions for the organization.

The power of the board also comes from the connections of human and non-human actors in the network of the board of directors. The network of the board is more extensive when we take into consideration the board members' families, investment, employment and education history, advisory role, and board and professional memberships. To illustrate how power is circulated in the network of the board, I show in Figure 4.2 the different connections of board members. They include familial and personal connections as well as professional and academic connections. For example, Larry Page is the CEO of Google and Alphabet, but he is also an investor of Tesla, a former student at Stanford University, and a member of the National Academy of Engineering. Sergey Brin is the President of Google, former husband of Anne Wojcicki, former student at Stanford University, donor of the Brin Wojcicki Foundation, and a member of the National Academy of Engineering. After finding out the first level of connections, I also looked at the second level of connections. For example, who sits on the Board of Trustees of Stanford University? Who belongs to the family of Anne Wojcicki?

Figure 4.2 shows what an extended network of the board looks like. The network consists of both individuals and organizations. Individuals include the directors, their family members, and former colleagues. Organizations include companies, universities, foundations, and professional associations. The larger the font size of the names, the more connections the actors have; the more connections of the actors have, the more powerful the actors are in the network. The network shows that although Larry Page and Sergey Brin are the founders of Google, three other individuals (Eric Schmidt, Anne Wojcicki, and Diane Greene) actually have more connections in the network. The power of Schmidt comes from his relationship with a number of universities and companies: he is an alumnus of Princeton University and University of California, Berkeley; he sits on the board of Princeton University; he was a CEO of Google and Alphabet, a former president of Sun Microsystems; and he is a member of the United States National Academy of Engineering.

Figure 4.2 Network of the Board of Directors.

Anne Wojcicki, former spouse of Sergey Brin, is a founder of 23andme (which was co-funded by Brin), a donor to the Brin Wojcicki Foundation, and an alumna of Yale University. Diane Greene, an Alphabet board member, was educated at the University of California, Berkeley, and the Massachusetts Institute of Technology; she is on the board of Intuit (a software company); and is a member of the National Academy of Engineering.

However, the most surprising finding revealed from the network is that there are few prominent organizations in the network of Google's board of directors. If we don't count Google and Alphabet, the most prominent organizations in the network are universities (Harvard University, Stanford University, and the Massachusetts Institute of Technology in particular), the venture capitalist firm Kleiner Perkins, and the professional association the National Academy of Engineering. These organizations are highly selective of their members, who tend to belong to more than one of these organizations. For example, the three universities admit less than 10% of outstanding applicants to their undergraduate programs. Kleiner Perkins, based in Silicon Valley, seeks interns from nearby University of California, Berkeley, and

Stanford University. Membership of the National Academy of Engineering is by election by its members. Faculty members from prominent universities have a much better chance of being nominated and elected than those from less prominent institutions.

The network of Google's board shows the meritocratic nature of the hi-tech industry (also see Chapter 5, "Cultural Profile"). Google may appear to be an egalitarian company because it provides "free" services to literate populations with Internet access and because its services are relatively easy to use. However, those who make decisions for the masses are connected to only a limited number of highly selective organizations such as elite colleges and national associations.

Government Advisory Role, Campaign Contribution, and Lobbying

Another network in which power reproduces and circulates is Alphabet's relationship with the government. This relationship can be both formal and informal. Information about the formal relationship is more readily available in the name of corporate transparency. Information about informal relationships is harder to discover because it may come from speculation and hearsay. For example, Julian Assange (2014), the founder of WikiLeaks, suggested that Google is like a pseudo-government that directly interferes with international relations with foreign governments. He came into this conclusion after meeting with the former Google CEO, Eric Schmidt, and Google Ideas (now called Google Jigsaw) director, Jared Cohen. Assange wrote a book that provided the transcript of a conversation between him, Schmidt, and Cohen. He suggested that Schmidt and Cohen, with their friendly relationship with the US government, share intelligence information gathered from online activities. Although Assange is transparent about the meeting, the subtext of the conversation can be interpreted in different ways. Because Assange is wary of the lack of online privacy, he arrived at a speculative relationship between Alphabet and the US government. Informal relationships such as this can hardly be verified or quantified because of their speculative nature.

Government Advisory Role

This section only concerns the formal relationship between Alphabet and the US government, information that can be verified and quantified. The three kinds considered here are governmental advisory roles, campaign contributions, and lobbying efforts.

Alphabet's relationship with the US government can be characterized as friendly, especially during the eight years of the Obama administration (2009–2016).[5] Before Obama was elected to be president, he made a trip to

Google headquarters to meet with employees (Stross, 2007). When Obama was elected for the first term, Eric Schmidt served as an adviser to the president. The White House record also showed that Schmidt made 18 trips to the White House, including 4 1-on-1 meetings with the president.[6] In 2016, Schmidt agreed to co-chair an advisory board for the Pentagon with former president Jimmy Carter (Shalal, 2016).

Campaign Donation

Like most technology companies, Google employees tend to be supporters of the Democratic Party in the US (Wilson, 2016). For the first term of Obama, Google employees generously donated to the presidential campaign. Only employees in two corporations, Goldman Sachs and Microsoft, gave more to a campaign than Googlers (Yang & Easton, 2009). For Obama's re-election, only employees of two organizations gave more than Googlers to the campaign: the University of California and Microsoft. In 2018, about 81 percent of the donations of Google's employees went to the Democrats; they gave $4.6 million to all campaigns;[7] $1.6 million was also given to campaigns by political action committees (PACs). Despite the amount, Alphabet's contribution by PACs was not as significant as that of others: it was not one of the top 20 donors. PACs can also be formed by business organizations, labor unions, and ideological groups.

Lobbying

Lobbying is another formal relationship that a corporation can establish with the government. Alphabet hires lobbyists to influence politicians and government agencies on a wide range of issues from self-driving cars and immigration to tax reform. Even though Alphabet prides itself on doing things differently, when it comes to lobbying, it acts like a conventional corporation. In fact, it was the largest government lobbyist in the US in 2017 (Shaban, 2018). According to *Fortune* (Bach, 2018), the company spent $18 million that year on swaying politicians' opinions. It was the second most generous government lobbyist; it only spent one million dollars less than AT&T, but spent more than Comcast (media and telecommunications) and Amazon.com (online retailers).[8] Google has an office in Washington, DC, that primarily focuses on lobbying.

What kinds of public issues does Alphabet spend money on? According to OpenSecrets.org, the company has filed more than ten reports in the following nine areas: (1) labor, antitrust, and workplace; (2) copyright, patent, and trademark; (3) consumer product safety; (4) telecommunications; (5) trade; (6) science and technology; (7) homeland security; (8) immigration; and (9) computers and information technology. Along with Alphabet, another 38 companies have lobbied on these nine issues. While some companies are in information technologies business like Alphabet, others are not.

In Figure 4.3, I singled out the top ten organizations that filed the most reports under the nine issues. They include: Cigna (healthcare insurance), Amazon.com, Pandora Music (music streaming), Spotify (music streaming) as well as Uber Technologies (car-sharing). Those who have filed issues about trade include Exxon Mobile (energy), Nike (sports apparel and equipment), eBay (online auction), FedEx (courier), Walmart (retail), Boeing (transportation), General Electric (energy, financial), Intel (computing), and Pepsi (consumer products).

Trade groups, professional groups, and labor unions also lobby the government. Trade groups are big spenders on the same lobbying issues that concern Alphabet. The 13 trade groups represent industries such as hospitality, retail, franchise, and medicine. Some of these trade groups represent industries that are hostile toward Alphabet. For example, the Motion Picture Association of America (MPAA) and the Recording Industry Association of America (RIAA) believe that Google Search and YouTube made copyrighted media readily available.

Professional associations, labor unions, and education institutions also lobby government on issues, but they do not file as many reports as business organizations and trade associations. They also spend less on lobbying. The only labor union that lobbied on issues that also concerned Alphabet was the Teamsters Union, which represents a large number of workers in different industries ranging from food and beverage and transport to the media. The only education institution that lobbied on issues that concerned Alphabet was Purdue University.

Figure 4.3 shows a network of relations through lobbying in 2018. The overwhelming number of lines mean that most lobbying reports were filed by corporations. The thinnest lines mean that the second most active lobbyists were trade groups. The dots on the outskirts are lobbying issues (labor, antitrust and workplace; copyright, patent and trademark; consumer product safety; telecommunications; trade; science and technology; homeland security; immigration; and computers and information technology). The thickest lines that go from the center to the dot in the top left corner show the large number of reports filed on telecommunications issues. Alphabet was subdued in their effort on lobbying telecommunications issues when compared to the largest corporate players (such as AT&T, Comcast, T-Mobile, and Verizon) and trade groups (such as The Internet and Television Association),

In addition to lobbying politicians' offices on specific issues, corporations also lobby the legislative and executive branches, such as the US Senate, the US House of Representatives, the White House, and the Executive

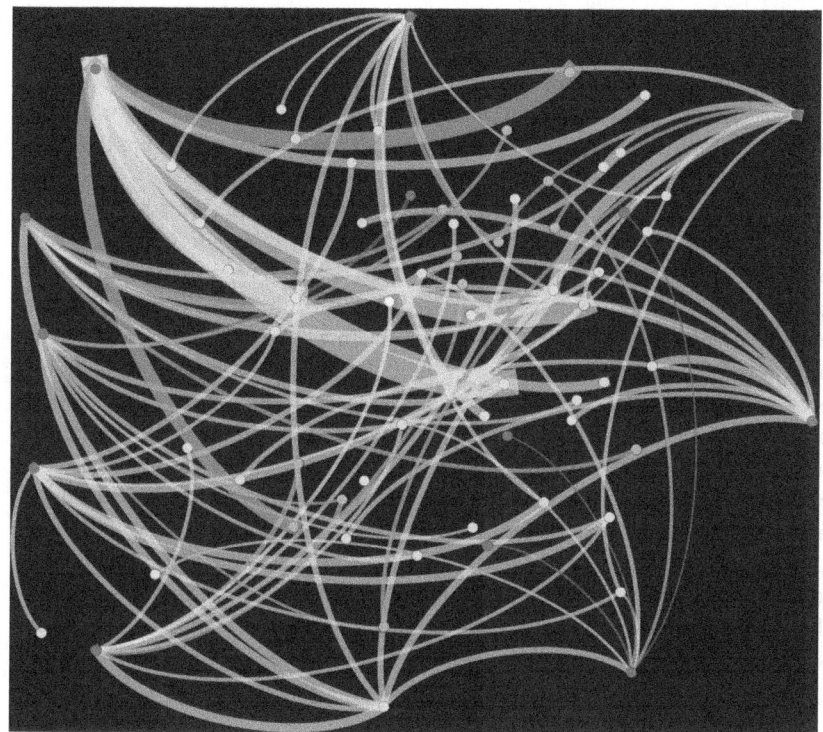

Figure 4.3 Lobbying from Corporations, Trade Groups, Professional Associations, Labor Unions, and Education Institutions.

Office of the President. Corporations can also lobby for specific bills. In 2018, Alphabet lobbied for 49 bills, among which are a few that are dear to Alphabet's businesses, such as HR 3388 SELF DRIVE Act that advocated for the enactment of federal laws to ensure the safety of "self-driving" cars.

Google in Other Countries

The equivalent to Google's cozy relationship with the US government is not found in two other of the world's large economies: The European Union (EU) and China. The EU has successfully fined Alphabet twice for antitrust violation. In 2017, the EU fined Alphabet for giving priority to Google Shopping over its competitors. When users search for a product, they often find it on Google Shopping rather than on other sites because the Google algorithm favors its own site than rival sites (Lomas, 2017). In 2018, EU once again fined Alphabet for antitrust violation. It found Alphabet bundling its applications with the Android operating system (see Chapter 3, "Economic Profile"), forcing users to favor the Google search engine and Chrome applications. The EU also sued Alphabet for not allowing competitors to run devices on different versions of Android. Lastly, it fined Alphabet for paying manufacturers and cell phone operators to bundle Google search applications on handsets (Warren, 2018).

Google's relationship with China is even rockier: the five brief years of Google in China has not only given rise to questions about Google's "don't be evil" motto, but it has also tested Google's belief in organizing the world's information. The unfortunate fate of Google in China was documented in a number of books for the popular market (such as Levy, 2011) so I will only offer a brief summary here. In 2005, Google decided to have a more visible presence in China, and it hired a former Microsoft employee Kai-fu Lee to be the president of Google China. It built a research and development center in Beijing and hired top talents. Not all Google employees in the US were enthusiastic about Google being in China, because of the country's records of human rights violation. Co-founder Sergey Brin who grew up in the Soviet Union was especially skeptical of countries with state-controlled media systems. US companies know that e-mail providers and search engine companies that operate in China are expected to comply with the Chinese government to hand over private information and users' data. For example, the Chinese government has, in the past, asked Yahoo! to share e-mails of political dissidents—who were later prosecuted by the Chinese government. Google setting up shop in China then appeared to do more evil than less. However, the company believed that the Chinese market was too big to miss and that the company could continue with its mission of providing information to the most people (McLaughlin, 2006). A few years in China showed that Google had failed on both counts. First, the company never gained a large market share. It was more popular among the well-educated elites in big cities, but the majority of the population preferred the homegrown search engine Baidu. Second, before Google could liberate Chinese citizens, Google e-mail accounts of political dissidents were hacked into. Google suspected the hackers were not amateurs who were simply testing the security of Google, but government employees who were instructed to break into e-mail accounts of activists to show Google the power of the government. Google withdrew from China in 2010, less than five years after its high-profile landing in the country.

From a political economic perspective, corporations and governments are seen to engage in power struggles. The US government is generally seen to be more friendly with large corporations. Even though Google is constrained by laws such as antitrust and fair use, its monopoly power in Internet search and e-mails is less challenged in the US. Political economists such as

McChesney (1999) critique the cozy relationship between the US government and corporations. Together they maintain the power held by elites, leaving the consumers with few choices. The European Union, in general, is seen to be less friendly with big corporations. The lawsuits against Google show that Europeans have less tolerance for monopoly power. The Chinese government is yet more hostile toward foreign media corporations and information companies. The fact that Google had to comply with the Chinese government's censorship rules shows that US corporations have much less power in China than in the US.

A political economic critique assumes that both corporations and governments are stable entities, and that power struggles occur when these entities compete for control. From this perspective, Google is a singular entity regardless of its sites of operation in the US, the European Union, or the Chinese market. The power of Google is believed to carry over from one market to another *unless* the appropriate government stops it from exercising that power. In this sense, Google in Europe and China is inherently powerful because power is transferred from the parent company in the US to the overseas markets. In the same vein, governments are seen as monolithic entities that exercise power *on* corporations and citizens as well as regulate the power relations *between* corporations and citizens.

From an Actor-Network Theory perspective, Google and governments are unstable entities. Corporations and governments are both networks made up of human and non-human actors, which are in a constant motion of connecting with and disconnecting from each other. Google's expansion into China was less about a transplant of a powerful entity from one country to another, and more about an emerging network that is in still in formation. Human actors (such as Google executives hired by the headquarters in the US and Chinese engineers trained in elite universities) and non-human actors (such as Google's algorithm, Chinese intellectual property laws, or Chinese government protocols for Internet companies) are connected in the network that also prompts actors to behave in a certain way. For example, the Google search algorithm in China evolved in response to government officials' instructions. From a network perspective, Google Search in China was not necessarily superior or inferior to the one in the US because the algorithm would respond to the network in which it is created. However, users who believe the algorithm should only evolve in response to users' search behavior would find the Google China search engine to be inferior because it responded to political pressure. On the other hand, the Chinese government believed that the algorithm that responded to Internet protocol was superior because it actively responded to other non-human and human actors (such as Chinese media regulations and government officials).

Despite one type of network responding to users' behavior and the other responding to Internet protocols, power is produced and circulated through the connections between actors in both types of networks. The algorithm of Google Search in the US is seen as powerful because it gathers information about how users search and with what keywords searches are conducted. The algorithm then responds to aggregated data by providing users with "relevant" information. The search engine in China is equally powerful because government officials can write Internet protocols to influence search results, and they can also obtain information from search companies about users' behaviors. From an ANT perspective, the case of Google in China is not about whether Google or the Chinese government was more powerful, but it is about how networks behaved because of the connections between different actors.

Political Profile: What is Google?

Alphabet is said to be a powerful entity and the co-founders are said to be powerful people. For example, *Forbes* ranked Larry Page and Sergey Brin as the 10th and 35th most powerful people, respectively, in the world in 2018.[9] The magazine did not explain what power is but it gave evidence about what power looks like: it means leading and co-founding Google, inventing an algorithm, having a lot of money, and being a "game changer". Political economists may differ from *Forbes* by being critical of how powerful people become powerful at the expense of others, yet they also tend to believe that power resides with entities, whether they are organizations or individuals. This assumption is flawed because it ignores the networks that create and generate power as do the non-human actors in the networks.

This chapter challenges political economists to think about power differently: it asks them to think that power is generated in networks constituted of human and non-human actors. Networks such as the stock markets, boards of directors, and lobbying are not only made up of individuals, but they are also made up of non-human actors, such as technologies and technical devices. Human and non-human actors exert power on each other: while traders use the computer to trade Alphabet stocks on Nasdaq, the stock prices generated by the computer also prompt the traders to act; while the boards of directors make decisions about hiring and firing executives, the bylaws also constrain what they can do with regard to the executive board.

The power of Alphabet came from the connections that it established in the stock market, the board of directors, and the government. I have shown that tech start-ups are expected to hold IPOs and to connect themselves with the stock market to generate more capital. By becoming a public company, Google tapped into more resources via the stock market. However, being in a stock market also constrains Google's direction because the institutional owners that hold a large number of Alphabet stocks can influence the company's decisions. Alphabet cannot *not* continuously grow because its performance is directly tied to that of institutional owners. Google in China is an example that demonstrates the company's hunger to grow (also see Chapter 3, "Economic Profile"). However, human and non-human actors are configured differently in the network in China so Google Search failed to operate in the same way as in other countries. Google's withdrawal from China may not necessarily mean the Chinese government has more power than Google, it only means that the power is distributed differently in the network from the way Google had anticipated. In this sense, the network concept will shift political economists' attention from discussing the negative outcomes of power to the generation and distribution of power.

Notes

1 https://x.company/projects/loon/
2 Choosing the right listing. NYSE. www.nyse.com/get-started/international/choosing-the-right-listing
3 GDP, current prices. IMF DataMapper. www.imf.org/external/datamapper/NGDPD@WEO/OEMDC/ADVEC/WEO/JPN/FRA
4 Amended and restated bylaws of Alphabet Inc. (October 2, 2015). https://abc.xyz/investor/pdf/amended_and_restated_bylaws.pdf
5 Barack Obama (D). OpenSecrets.org. www.opensecrets.org/pres12/contrib.php?id=N00009638. Accessed: 12th November, 2018.
6 "Eric Schmidt: Obama's chief corporate ally". Google Transparency Project. www.googletransparencyproject.org/articles/eric-schmidt-obamas-chief-corporate-ally. Accessed: 12th November, 2018.
7 Total contributions by party of recipient. Alphabet. OpenSecrets.org: Center for Responsive Politics. www.opensecrets.org/orgs/totals.php?id=D000067823&cycle=2018. Accessed: 20th November, 2018.
8 Top spenders. OpenSecrets.org: Center for Responsive Politics. www.opensecrets.org/lobby/top.php?showYear=2017&indexType=s. Access: 14th November, 2018.
9 "The world's most powerful people". *Forbes.* www.forbes.com/profile/larry-page/?list=powerful-people#5637e6e47893. Accessed: 14th January, 2019.

Bibliography

Assange, J. (2014). *When Google Met WikiLeaks*. New York: OR Books.
Bach, N. (2018, January 24). Google outspent every other company on Washington lobbying last year. *Fortune*. Retrieved from: http://fortune.com/2018/01/24/google-facebook-amazon-apple-lobbying-efforts/. Accessed: 14th November, 2018.
Barthes, R. (2012). *Mythologies*. New York: Hill and Wang. (Original published 1957).
Bilić, P. (2018). A critique of the political economy of algorithms: A brief history of Google's technological rationality. *Triple C: Cognition, Communication, Co-operation, 16*(1), 315–331.

Callon, M. (2007). An essay on the growing contribution of economic markets to the proliferation of the social. *Theory, Culture, and Society*, *24*(7/8), 139–163.

Callon, M., & Law, J. (1995). Agency and the hybrid collectif. *South Atlantic Quarterly*, *94*, 481–507.

Couldry, N. (2005). Actor network theory and media: Do they connect and on what terms? In: A. Hepp, S. Moores, & C. Winter (Eds.), *Connectivity, networks and flows: Conceptualizing contemporary communication* (pp. 93–110). Cresskill, NJ: Hampton Press.

Davis, G. F. (2009). *Managed by markets: How finance re-shaped America*. Oxford, UK: Oxford University Press.

Fine, B. (2005). From actor-network theory to political economy. *Capitalism Nature Socialism*, *16*(4), 91–108.

Foucault, M. (1971). *The order of things: An archeology of the human sciences*. New York: Pantheon.

Fuchs, C. (2011). *Foundations of critical media and information studies*. Oxford, UK: Routledge.

Gareau, B. J. (2005). We have never been human: Agential nature, ANT, and Marxist political ecology. *Capitalism Nature Socialism*, *16*(4), 127–140.

Gordon, J. S. (1999). *The great game: The emergence of Wall Street as a world power 1653–2000*. New York: Scribner.

Jeanneney, J.-N. (2007). *Google and the myth of universal knowledge: A view from Europe*. Chicago, IL: University of Chicago Press.

Latour, B. (2005). *Reassembling the social: An introduction to actor-network theory*. Oxford, UK: Oxford University Press.

Lee, M. (2014). What can political economists learn from economic sociologists? A case study of NASDAQ. *Communication, Culture, and Critique*, *7*(2), 246–263.

Levy, S. (2011). *In the plex: How Google thinks, works, and shapes our lives*. New York: Simon & Schuster.

Lomas, N. (2017, June 27). Google fined $2.7bn for EU antitrust violations over shopping searches. *TechCrunch*. Retrieved from: https://techcrunch.com/2017/06/27/google-fined-e2-42bn-for-eu-antitrust-violations-over-shopping-searches/. Accessed: 20th November, 2018.

McChesney, R. (1999). *Rich media, poor democracy: Communication politics in dubious times*. Urbana, IL: University of Illinois Press.

McChesney, R. (2014). *Digital disconnect*. New York: New Press.

McLaughlin, A. (2006, January 27). Google in China. The official Google blog. Retrieved from: https://googleblog.blogspot.com/2006/01/google-in-china.html. Accessed: 3rd April, 2019.

Mosco, V. (2004). *The digital sublime: Myth, power, and cyberspace*. Cambridge, MA: MIT Press.

Mosco, V. (2009). *The political economy of communication* (2nd ed.). London: Sage.

Noble, S. U. (2018). *Algorithms of oppression: How search engines reinforce racism*. New York: New York University Press.

Segev, E. (2010). *Google and the digital divide: The bias of online knowledge*. Oxford, UK: Chandes.

Shaban, H. (2018, January 23). Google for the first time outspent every other company to influence Washington in 2017. *Washington Post*. Retrieved from: www.washingtonpost.com/news/the-switch/wp/2018/01/23/google-outspent-every-other-company-on-federal-lobbying-in-2017/?utm_term=.f6542cd7730b. Accessed: 20th November, 2018.

Shalal, A. (2016, March 2). Former Google CEO Eric Schmidt is now on military advisory board for the Pentagon. *Business Insider*. Retrieved from: www.business insider.com/former-google-ceo-eric-schmidt-to-head-pentagon-innovation-board. Accessed: 12th November, 2018.

Stoller, K. (2018, May 9). Apple, Berkshire Hathaway lead America's largest public companies in 2018. *Forbes*. Retrieved from: www.forbes.com/sites/kristinstoller/2018/05/09/americas-largest-public-companies-2018/#513cbc6f1e1a. Accessed: 2nd April, 2019.

Stross, R. (2007, December 2). For the 2008 race, Google is a crucial constituency. *New York Times*. Retrieved from: www.nytimes.com/2007/12/02/business/02digi. html. Accessed: 12th November, 2018.

Vaidhyanathan, S. (2011). *The googlization of everything: And why we should worry*. Oakland, CA: University of California Press.

Warren, T. (2018, July 18). Google fined a record $5 billion by the EU for Android antitrust violations. *The Verge*. Retrieved from: www.theverge.com/2018/7/18/17580694/google-android-eu-fine-antitrust. Accessed: 20th November, 2018.

Wilson, M. R. (2016, June 7). Tech cash skews to Democrats. *The Hill*. Retrieved from: https://thehill.com/business-a-lobbying/business-a-lobbying/282418-tech-cash-skews-to-democrats. Accessed: 20th November, 2018.

Winseck. D. (2016). Reconstructing the political economy of communication for the digital media age. *The Political Economy of Communication*, 4(2), 73–114.

Yang, J. L. & Easton, N. (2009, October 26). Obama and Google (A love story). *Fortune*. Retrieved from: http://archive.fortune.com/2009/10/21/technology/obama_google.fortune/index.htm. Accessed: 12th November, 2018.

5 Cultural Profile

Alphabet primarily sees itself as a technology company that invents tools for users to produce content. Unlike media corporations, Alphabet is not viewed as a content producer, therefore it does not appear to be a company that creates culture. Technological tools are very often seen as value-free, they are believed to wait passively to be appropriated and adapted by users. To give a simple example, a pencil is seen as a dead object with no embedded culture until a person uses it to create cultural artifacts, such as writing great literature or sketching drawings. The pencil, however, embodies a person's writing culture, it bears a person's desire to externalize thoughts. From an Actor-Network Theory perspective, technical objects are not passive, they probe human beings to interact with them. Non-human objects also enable humans to do things that are impossible without them.

If a humble pencil is not value-free, then tools such as Google Docs, the Android operating system, and Google Maps are definitely not value-free, they embody the culture of the organization within which they were invented. I argue in this chapter that Alphabet exhibits an engineer-dominated culture that prides itself on data-driven problem-solving. Historically, even though there had been firms that hired a large number of engineers, Alphabet's engineer-dominated corporate culture is seen as new because the Internet infrastructure that enables the company's becoming is believed to usher in a new era. Companies that rely and thrive on the Internet are automatically assumed to be iconoclasts of old corporate culture. Management style in these new corporations is believed to do away with old-fashioned practices such as the "old boy" network, suit-and-tie attire, cubicles, and business lunches.

However, I argue that an engineer-dominated culture promotes a meritocracy ideology that is blind to gender, race, and class. This ideology believes that meritocracy is fair and democratic because decisions are made based solely on objective criteria such as technical skills and intellect. Therefore, meritocracy shapes the Alphabet workforce from hiring and promotion to compensation. When meritocracy is treated as a principle rather than a culture, an engineer-dominated culture is *naturalized* to be value-free.

This naturalized culture not only tolerates bias toward gender, race, and class, but it also perpetuates what old corporate culture produces: White male privilege. This privilege surfaced in 2018 when the *The New York Times* published a series of damaging articles about how Alphabet tolerates sexual harassment in the company (Wakabayashi & Conger, 2018). Following media reports of sexual harassment were those of workplace inequities: the disparities of compensation and benefits enjoyed by permanent and contract workers. Employee-activists also drew attention to the marginalization and job segregation of women of color in the organization. The high-profile grievances show that meritocracy does not necessarily solve the problems of the old corporate world, instead it reproduces them in different forms. For example, while women traders in the stock markets are said to be not aggressive enough, women engineers in hi-tech firms are said to be not technical enough. In this chapter, I examine how Alphabet's engineer-dominated culture promotes the meritocracy ideology through hiring, job segregation, and work inequities.

Does Alphabet Have a Culture?

Unlike content companies, such as Disney, Alphabet does not have memorable cultural icons such as Mickey Mouse or the princesses. The most memorable cultural image it offers is probably the Google logo and the sparse home page of Google Search. However, the Google logo is not as universally recognized as Mickey Mouse. To populations who do not go online or to those who prefer to use other search engines and online services, the logo may not mean much. However, Alphabet, along with other companies that would not have existed without the Internet, has created an online culture that has become a way of life for populations who have access to a computer and/or mobile phones. The Internet, along with infrastructure such as clean water and electricity, has become a part of modern life to such an extent that it is difficult to imagine life without it.

Are the Internet, clean water, and electricity culture? Can technology be culture? If culture is defined as a set of beliefs and values, practices and rituals, judgments and orientations, then most people in developed economies live in a technology culture without thinking too much about it. In a way, online culture is like American culture or Jewish culture—people who live in a culture treat it as the most natural way of life. They rarely question the culture unless they are removed from it and begin to see it in a new light, such as living abroad or converting to a new religion. Similarly, populations who are used to online culture may feel "disconnected" from the world when there is no Wi-Fi or cellular connection.

However, unlike American or Jewish culture, which are passed down by older generations and cultivated in communities, online culture is dominated by private interests. While it is undeniable that American culture is also fostered by commercial enterprises, it is hard to suggest that corporations such as Coca-Cola and McDonald's dominate the entire American culture. It is even harder to suggest family-owned Jewish delis dominate the entire Jewish culture. In contrast, online culture is dominated by corporations, not community groups or the government. According to Alexa.com,[1] the top ten websites frequented by online users in December 2018 were, all except one, owned by corporations: Google, YouTube (owned by Google), Facebook, Baidu, Wikipedia, Qq, Amazon, Taobao, Yahoo, and Tmail. Because online culture is fostered by corporations that rely on the Internet for their existence, they need to encourage users to feel this way of life is superior and to persuade them to stay. What characterizes this online culture fostered by Alphabet and other hi-tech corporations? I argue that this online culture is seen as new and future-oriented. It does not look back at tradition, it frowns at convention, and despises everything of the past. The focus on "newness" is shown in Alphabet's organizational culture that creates more services and tools to promote online culture. Online culture marks a sharp break from old culture; it is not seen as a gradual improvement upon the old, but it seeks to replace it.

Organizational culture is defined as "a system of shared assumptions, values, and beliefs that show people what is appropriate and inappropriate behavior" (Principles of management, 2010, Chapter 8, para. 1). Organizational culture influences employees' behavior. Hi-tech companies such as Facebook, Amazon.com, and Netflix are often said to have a lateral organizational structure, relaxing work environment, and youthful spirit. Alphabet, like some of its peers, is seen to be different from large, "traditional" corporations such as investment banks, automobile companies, and energy suppliers. A piece of evidence to show Google's supposedly non-hierarchical organizational structure is the use of shared offices. One often-recited tale is that when Eric Schmidt was hired to be the CEO in 2001, he found himself sharing an office with an engineer (Levy, 2011). At that time, Schmidt was already a Silicon Valley veteran and a millionaire, so having him share an office seems to suggest that Google fosters an egalitarian culture in which every employee is equally valued. In addition, as shown in Chapter 2, "History", colorful and quirky office decor at the Alphabet headquarters is often mentioned to reflect the unusualness of this company. Unlike the lobby of investment bank buildings, Alphabet does not favor marble columns and gold elevator doors. It is, however, partial to colorful furniture and old CPU units. The Alphabet headquarters' campus is often said to remind visitors that they are on a college campus: casual dress code, healthy food choices, onsite gym, and massage room—all catering to the employees' youthful orientation.

What If the New Has Never Been New?

Mosco (2004) argued that computer communication technology still holds a mythical status in society, in the same way that electricity and radio once did. The myth "the Internet is new" leads to an uncritical embrace from society even though counter-evidence exists to challenge this newness. Drawing on Barthes' concept of myth (1972/1957), Mosco argued that myth asks us to believe digital technology is something new, something that produces a break in history. The myth of digital technology maintains the story "about how even smaller, faster, cheaper, and better computer and communication technologies help to realize, with little effort, those seemingly impossible dreams of democracy and community with practically no pressure on the natural environment" (Mosco, 2004, p. 30). The belief in newness in technology leads to yet other beliefs: we are no longer living in a world of scarcity, but a world of abundance; we are no longer doing manual work that requires brawn, but mental work that requires brain; we are no longer bounded by traditions, but are free to choose fate and destiny.

Alphabet, along with other technology companies, is a poster boy for the "new" digital technology that has overcome the limitations of scarcity (see Chapter 3, "Economic Profile"). According to *Forbes*, the three most admired companies in the world are Apple, Amazon, and Alphabet. Alphabet received high scores on people management, social responsibility, quality of management, financial soundness, long-term investment value, and global competitiveness.[2] The high scores seem to confirm that Alphabet has found ways to conquer the struggles between workers and shareholders, private interests and the common good, and profits and social responsibilities. Technology is assumed to ease the tensions between various stakeholders that characterize old industries.

This myth seems to have been questioned of late when some of Alphabet's decisions led to a massive employee walkout and the European Union's lawsuits (see Chapter 4, "Political Profile"). Problematic decisions also trouble other technology companies, such as Facebook, for example, for permitting false information to interfere with democratic processes, Amazon.com favoring its own brands on the online site, and Apple using vendors that have little regard for workers' physical and mental health. Is it possible that the new has become old, or is it possible that the new has never been new? One popular explanation to these ill-advised decisions is that when Alphabet became bigger, it lost the core value "don't be evil" (Levy, 2011). In other words, as a company "matures", it tends to follow a conventional path. I propose another explanation here: what if Alphabet has never been new and future-oriented? What if the "newness" of Alphabet is built on the supposed "newness" of the Internet on which Alphabet capitalizes? What if the Internet is not entirely new, but a continuation of an unequal political-economic structure? What if the human and non-human actors associated with the Internet are not entirely new, but a reconfiguration of the actors? The Internet, the online culture, and Alphabet are only said to be new because the discourse about them exerts a force on the network in which human actors pick up the network attributes of being and acting "new". In the following, I examine how the discourse of Alphabet's hiring produces the ideology of meritocracy that is supposed to be blind to gender and race. The discourse, in turn, acts on prospective and current employees making them believe their privilege is rightfully deserved because of their merits, not because of their race or gender.

How Do Engineers See the World? Symbolic Universe and Ideology

One aspect of this "newness" is that Alphabet is an engineer-driven corporate culture. This culture is particularly celebrated in the popular press that caters for readers who are interested in the business of technology. For example, in Levy's (2011) extensive study of Google, he wrote that the company approaches all problems from an engineering perspective. This approach is seen to be superior to a business executive-driven culture. For example, when Google decided to cut costs during the recession, instead of hiring expensive business consultants like other corporations, Google gathered its employees together to brainstorm ideas. Innovative solutions were said to have been generated from the crowd wisdom and resulted in, for example, the closing of one of the less-frequented cafeterias and using smaller food portions. In another instance, a newly hired project manager was frustrated at engineers not listening to him. The founders' response to the new hire is that the project manager should listen to the engineers, not the other way round. Levy concluded that Google is different from conventional corporations because the worldview of engineers is more objective and data-driven.

While it is unavoidable that a company with a large number of engineers will have an engineer-dominated culture, this culture is cultivated in order to achieve the profit-making goals of the corporation. The engineers are not asked to solve any problems regardless of political-economic consequences. In addition, when a large and influential corporation like Alphabet promotes an engineer-dominated culture as superior, this culture may influence other organizations in other industries to adopt such a culture. For example, a former Google engineer, Sep Kamvar, founded "micro-schools" around the country by borrowing some engineering principles of the network.[3] On the webpage, it wrote that the schools' approach to education "led us to open-source the model". In the schools, the teacher-leader is linked by "a network of shared relationships" ("Wildflower Schools", para. 1). The network of the schools build and rely on what Benkler (2006) calls the wealth of the network:

> As we grow, we benefit from an expanding community of learners and professionals working together, and the *economic efficiencies* that can arise from *sharing resources* ... we resist the expansion of *central-administration* and *authority* ... each school sees itself as a *node in a network* ... we make our *materials, software and learnings available publicly*, so that all schools can benefit from them, whether or not they are affiliated with Wildflower.
>
> ("Wildflower Schools", para. 9, emphasis added)

Not mentioned on the micro-school's website is that teachers in each of the "nodes" collect data about students' learning, and those data are shared with the founder who works at the famed Media Lab at the Massachusetts Institute of Technology (Noonoo, 2018). The fast growth of the school network (from a handful to more than 20 within a year) may show that the "Googlization" of school networks gained some traction among parents who seek an alternative to public schools. The acceptance of micro-schools as a network may be influenced by an acceptance of engineer-dominated culture.

Who are Googlers?

How is the engineer-dominated corporate culture fostered in Alphabet? What are some implications of this engineer-dominated culture? I discuss three implications here: first, aspiring Googlers are required to think like Googlers. Candidates need to act like Googlers even before they are hired because Google engineer jobs are seen as some of the most prestigious and well-paid ones in the industry. Second, an engineer-dominated corporate culture reinforces the divide between engineers, other white-collar workers, and manual workers. Job stratification runs against Google's ideal of benefiting the greatest number of users. Third, but not least, the engineer-dominated culture legitimizes White males, who have traditionally held the most power in US society, as the default leaders of the company. Because Alphabet hiring emphasizes culture fit, candidates who are identified and perceived as non-male, non-White/Asian may have a harder time convincing the hiring managers that they share Google culture. Alphabet's emphasis on hiring the best engineers accentuates the lack of diversity in the engineering field. The small pool of non-male, non-White/Asian engineers may not produce as much cream of the crop when compared to the large pool of White male and Asian male candidates.

Many sources have related that, when Google started out, the founders insisted on vetting the candidates themselves (Levy, 2011). In addition to engineering caliber, the potential hirees also have to be a culture fit. Many accounts have also mentioned that the founders preferred candidates— regardless of their positions—with an engineering to a business background because the founders were not too keen on being lectured on business jargon and best business practices. One anecdote that illustrates this is when the earliest investors insisted on hiring a CEO, the founders rejected a number of Silicon Valley veterans for not being a culture fit. They eventually settled on Eric Schmidt because, as said, he was trained as an engineer and had gone to the Burning Man Festival. While the criteria for Brin and Page to select a CEO seems to be quirky, they show that Alphabet has an explicit cultural bias toward hiring. Similar to the many criticisms of the biased hiring of investment bankers (Roth, 2006), Alphabet hiring is also biased. The difference is that investment bankers recruit from exclusive networks associated with upper-class, male-oriented activities (such as golfing and hunting) and Alphabet recruits based on meritocracy and culture fit, such as graduates from computer science departments of elite universities.

The Google Jobs page tells aspiring employees what kind of culture they should fit into. Even though it stated that "there's no one kind of Googler", candidates should have "curiosity, passion, and desire to learn" and enjoy working with colleagues who are "big thinkers" and can "take on fresh challenges as a team". The language used to describe the ideal Googlers is similar to that for ideal students in elite universities. For example, Stanford undergraduate students are said to, "create and apply knowledge by thinking and doing, preparing for leadership in a rapidly changing world".[4] Students from the California Institute of Technology are said to be "curious and passionate in one of the world's most rigorous academic environments".[5] In contrast, such language is not found in community colleges that attract more low-income, first-generation, and immigrant students. For example, Foothill College, that is nine miles away from Stanford University, does not describe what an ideal student is. But it emphasizes "open enrollment", "[students] eligibility to have cost of tuition and fees waived", and "special programs to help you get started with college or ways to help you to pay for fees and books".[6] The starkly different languages show that the ideal students of elite universities, like Googlers, are asked to focus on ideas, not basic necessities. Students who are keen on learning but have to take care of daily necessities may find themselves better off at a place that meets daily life needs.

Because the ideal Googlers should think big and not worry about meeting basic needs, they are asked to think for themselves. Google Jobs asked candidates to highlight achievements, align skills and experience with the job description, state measurable outcomes of specific projects, and give examples of leadership. The ability to see oneself as a continuous self-improvement project (McRobbie, 2004) requires a certain kind of education and family background. Students who have a privileged educational background (such as preparatory schools, honors colleges, and elite universities) are more equipped to think about themselves as professionals. Students who attend community colleges may find themselves working manual service jobs to meet basic necessities.

Unlike Alphabet jobs, manual service jobs ask for manual labor and obedience. For example, In-n-out Burger that is in close proximity to Google's Mountain View campus requires workers to "move freely in and around obstacles common in the stores", "the use of all limbs and the ability to see at close distance", "follow directions", "interact productively with co-workers", "follow posted work rules and procedures", and "perform all work related tasks".[7] Similar to Google Jobs, the job descriptions of manual labor already prescribe the kinds of culture expected at a burger chain. Graduates of community colleges who are asked to think about obedience and basic needs may not find the Alphabet job description speaking to them.

Alphabet does not see all skills as equal, they privilege quantitative skills to people's skills, such as interpersonal and communication skills. Shortlisted candidates are asked to demonstrate coding competency. The interviewers are said to ask strictly technical questions and care little about social grace:

> Your phone interview will cover data structures and algorithms. Be prepared to write around 20–30 lines of code in your strongest language. Approach all scripting as a coding exercise—this should be *clean, rich, robust* code:
>
> 1 You will be asked an open ended question. Ask clarifying questions, devise requirements.
> 2 You will be asked to explain it in an algorithm.
> 3 Convert it to workable code. (Hint: Don't worry about getting it perfect because time is limited. Write what comes but then refine it later. Also make sure you consider corner cases and edge cases, production ready).
> 4 Optimize the code, follow it with test cases and find any bugs.
>
> (emphasis added)[8]

The description of what to expect in an interview is like a standardized testing preparation manual. Candidates who have jumped through hoops of standardized college admission testing will undoubtedly find the instruction culturally familiar. Google Jobs does not accept any good answer, it prescribes what the best answer should be like: the code should be "clean, rich, robust". The same page further describes subject areas with which the candidates should be familiar: coding, algorithms, sorting, data structures, mathematics, graphics, and recursion. To prepare candidates for the coding test, Google Jobs even suggested sites such as good online resources and self-practices on a Chromebook or a whiteboard.

Google Jobs further prescribes what an ideal Googler is. It listed that recruiters look at four areas: general cognitive ability, leadership, role-related knowledge, and "googleyness". "General cognitive ability" and "role-related knowledge" prescribe how engineers should think. Skills that candidates should demonstrate are: problem-solving, explaining thought process, data-driven decision-making, driving impact, inventing new roles in the future. Culture fit is measured by how "googleyness" a candidate is. An ideal candidate should "Share how you work individually and on a team, how you help others, how you navigate ambiguity, and how you push yourself to grow outside of your comfort zone".[9]

If the above is not specific enough, Google recruiters also want the candidates to prepare for the interview in extremely specific ways. For example, they are first asked to "google 'most common interview questions'"[10], predict the top 20 questions, then write down the answers and practice them at home. It then warned the candidates that the interviewer may not like the first answer so the interviewees should always prepare three answers hoping to hit the jackpot. Aspiring Googlers are already asked to learn the culture before they are hired. On the other side of the table, recruiters are also asked to seek hirees who fit very exact criteria.

The Cult of Getting Hired

Even though Google Jobs explain the process in details, the process of getting hired at Alphabet has become almost like a religious ritual on online discussion forums. Aspiring applicants want to know how difficult it is to get an interview and how they can get hired. When I typed in "how to get hired by Google", the search box already completed my query by adding keywords such as "Reddit" and "Quora" and suggesting popular search phrases such as "how hard and difficult it is to get hired by Google". The suggestions showed that many casual and serious aspiring Googlers have wondered about their chances.

On Quora,[11] aspiring Googlers asked, "How can I get a job at Facebook or Google in 6 months?"; "Should I quit my job and start learning algorithm and data structures to get a job in big companies like Google?"; "How do I start off to get a good job in Google/Facebook/Amazon, etc?". The responses usually reinforced the meritocratic belief that intellectual prowess, technical skills, and preparation are all one needs to get an offer from Alphabet. Respondents believed that when one's will is strong, it can overcome any difficulty. For instance, working for Alphabet should be the ultimate career, if not life, goal: "the only thing I wanted to do was work for Google". They then explained a rigorous self-imposed practice plan: "Day 1 – The Book; Days 2–14 – Algorithms stage; Days 14–24 Coding stage; Day 25 – Onto some questions; Days 26–30 Solving CareerCup questions; Day 30.5 – Skip lists (Google-only); Day 31 –The non-technical stuff". The hirees saw themselves as good raw materials that could be molded to become Google materials.

Online advice did not mention whether systematic discrimination and exclusion shaped by racial, gender, and class inequalities hinder ones' ability to practice the skills. For instance, the advice suggested that the best strategy is to study alone. For women and non-Asian minorities, they may prefer to study with others. There was also little advice on how one can make a living to meet basic needs while preparing for the Google interview full-time. The advice assumes that applicants have no financial constraints and can study for the interview as if it were a full-time job. Not working for money for a whole month is simply impossible for many adults in the US, if not worldwide.

The Online Culture of Being Rejected by Alphabet

Rejection by Google and other tech companies has become an online culture—there is a website dedicated to aspiring Googlers who did not get hired by Alphabet at We All Face Rejection (https://rejected.us). While sharing humbling experiences may appear like joining support groups such as Alcoholics Anonymous, posting on We All Face Rejection is not a step-by-step program to overcome hardship. In fact, the postings reinforce the belief in meritocracy: most of the messages imply that great talents will be recognized. The rejected candidates usually began the self-congratulatory notes by stating the number of rejections they received and the companies that have rejected them. And the notes usually ended with a resolution: they work at another well-known hi-tech company. Some examples are: "I was rejected from 10 unpaid internships. Now I work at Twitter"; "Couldn't even get a phone screen with Google or Twitter. Went on to work for Reddit and now Netflix"; "I was rejected without interview at Dropbox. Escorted out halfway through my Microsoft interview. Now I'm senior eng at Twitter". The entitled sense of meritocracy is shown by naming the parties that did not recognize their greatness. Some examples are: "rejected by MIT for undergrad, accepted to the computer science PhD program. (I chose Berkeley for grad school instead.)"; "I was at the University of Illinois at Urbana-Champaign for a year. […] I dropped out, and was almost immediately hired as a freelance contractor for a billion dollar investment company, and told that I could name my own price".

Judging from the profile pictures, the majority of the rejected candidates would identify themselves as younger White males. They did not reflect on whether their race, gender, and age would advance their career or hinder it. Those who brought up the idea that gender, race, and national origin may influence hiring decisions all identified themselves as non-White or non-male. For example, one person wrote "I was refused a reference by my supervisor […] who thought the male student on my team did all the work"; another wrote "before Twitter, I was rejected twice by bit tech co, which only interviewed me cuz I had scholarship they gave to Latino students"; "A swedish [sic] startup company dropped from skype [sic] mid call after I told them I was born in Turkey". No rejected candidate posted on the board how they coped with financial difficulties while studying for an interview or waiting for a job offer. Similar to the online forums that advise aspiring Googlers how to study for the interview, those who shared their rejection stories did not seem to explicate that financial struggles are real. For candidates who do not have the financial means to study for the interviews and wait for the perfect job, they may need to take whatever jobs they can get in order to pay bills.

Alphabet's economic power reinforces a meritocracy ideology among its employees and aspiring Googlers. Hiring overly emphasizes quantitative and technical skills, and these skills are believed to be perfected by applicants in their own time. The meritocracy ideology appears to be democratic: the numerous sites give a lot of information about how hiring is done and what kinds of questions are asked. However, the ideology fails to acknowledge that the emphasis on technical skills has a gender, race, and class bias because it masks structural inequalities in both the education system and the online culture. As computer science is predominately studied by White and Asian males, students who identify as women and/or non-White/non-Asian may feel they do not belong to the culture. According to the National Center for Education Statistics, in 2011, only 18 percent of college graduates with a computer science degree identified as women.[12] The small number of women and non-White/non-Asian computer science candidates in turn makes it appear that women and non-Whites/non-Asians do not have the technical skills to succeed at an engineering job. The unfortunate case of a former Google employee who circulated a letter insulting women's technical skills and intellect should not be seen as an isolated incident of gender bias (Ingram, 2018).

In contrast to political economists, ANT scholars do not believe that there is such a thing as structural inequality in education and the job market. They also do not believe there are asymmetrical relationships in a network. Furthermore, they do not want to explain why White and Asian male candidates tend to outnumber others in the computer science field. They would instead suggest that because human actors associate themselves and non-human actors (such as computing devices, user manuals, programming languages) in a network called "computer science", the network gives meaning to both kinds of actors. In other words, by subscribing to a certain discourse, the network enacts a world in which a certain way of talking and behaving forms the reality (Farias & Mutzel, 2015). To give an example, aspiring Googlers will read through online advice sites, read programming language manuals, and interact with the computer to increase their chances of being hired. By being in the network, the computer and online sites create the Ideal Googler who is believed to possess an objective set of criteria with which job seekers are compared.

The Foucauldian concept of discourse (1971) is similar to an actor-network: subjects in a discourse are asked to conform to certain behaviors and speeches in order to claim a certain subject-position. In an online environment frequented by Google job seekers and current employees, they have to subscribe to a discourse that privileges technical language rather than emotional language. The advice and tips are almost all about technical preparation, rather than appearance, etiquette, and affect. There is little advice about ensuring the appearance is professional, the handshake is firm, and the smile is confident. In fact, if job seekers use language that is deemed feminine and cutesy (such as OMG, lol) or ask questions that are deemed frivolous (such as personal appearance at the interviews), they may be mocked as unserious candidates, even if they have the technical skills to be a Googler.

Job Stratification Across Race and Gender

Alphabet is seen as a great company for employees—working for the company is believed to be as good as a job can be. Fuchs (2013) called Google employees the aristocrats of the service industry. Although Google engineers belong to the same industry as a store assistant at a burger chain, they enjoy a much higher salary, more job benefits, and greater prestige. The online job recruitment site, Glassdoor, analyzed workers' reviews of companies and ranked Google as the eighth best workplace in 2019 in the US (Gassam, 2019). As argued earlier in the chapter, because Alphabet is seen to be different from corporations from the old economy, Alphabet's workplace is automatically assumed to be equitable, open, and transparent *despite* the obvious exclusivity of Alphabet jobs.

In November 2018, 20,000 Alphabet employees walked out at a number of Alphabet sites across the globe. The collective marches highlighted two elephants in the room: one on sexual harassment, the other on work equity. In an open letter to Google CEO Sundar Pichai, the organizers wrote that, "Google routinely denies TVCs [temporary workers, vendors, and contractors] access to information that is relevant to our jobs and our lives" (Google

Walkout for Real Change, 2018, para. 2). Despite the company's mission to organize the world's information, the letter pointed out,

> The exclusion of TVCs from important communications and fair treatment is part of a system of institutional racism, sexism, and discrimination. TVCs are disproportionately people from marginalized groups who are treated as less deserving of compensation, opportunities, workplace protections, and respect.
>
> (para. 3)

The organizers continued that, despite Alphabet's profits, they have been hiring more contractors than Googlers. Contractors demanded Alphabet to put "an end to pay and opportunity inequity for TVCs" (para. 7) and to allow for "access to company-wide information on the same terms as full-time employees" (para. 8). The latter demand is especially ironic given Google's image as an open and transparent company.

In this section, I argue that Google's organizational culture is nothing "new", and job stratification is pronounced across gender and racial lines: women of color are very often at the bottom of the organization's hierarchy, while White men from a middle-class background are at the top. Women of color tend not to do technical work, and therefore earn the least—and are the most disposable. However, the meritocracy ideology once again blinds some employees into believing that gender and race have no influence in women of color being at the bottom of the hierarchy.

Google's Diversity Report Card

Google said it takes diversity seriously. On its page on diversity, the company stated that "Google's mission is to organize the world's information and make it universally accessible and useful. When we say we want to build for everyone, we mean everyone. To do that well, we need a workforce that's more representative of the users we serve".[13] But the gender and racial composition of Google's workforce clearly does not represent the world's population. The diversity report stated that about 31 percent of Google employees are female worldwide (Google did not disclose the percentage of female employees in the U.S. in the diversity report). In the US, more than half of the employees identify as White, 36 percent as Asian, and only slightly more than 6 percent identify as black, Latinx, or Native American. Compared to the entire US population, Asians are overly represented in the company (only close to 6 percent of the US population self-identify as Asian), thus making Whites less represented in Google (close to 77 percent of the entire US population self-identify as White) (Google, 2018). However, in the entire US population, 32 percent identify as black, Latinx, or Native American. What this means is the US population has five times more non-Whites/non-Asians than those in Google.[14] The racial composition of Google workers is also more White than the world population: three-quarters of the world population live in Asia and Africa and only 10 percent live in Europe. This is not to suggest that Asians who live in Asia are the same as Asian Americans who live in the US, but this does not discount the fact that the world's most popular search engine is dominated by a racial group that represents only one in ten people in the world.

Gender and racial disparities are more pronounced at the leadership level. The Google diversity report (Google, 2018) showed that nearly two-thirds of Google leaders identify as White, and close to three-quarters identify as male. What this means is that White males are more likely to lead the organization than other racial groups and females. Even though 36 percent of Google workers self-identify as Asian, only 26 percent are in leadership positions. In contrast, 53 percent of Google workers self-identify as White, but close to 67 percent of leadership positions are occupied by this racial group. The report did not explain why women and Asians do not advance to leadership positions at a similar rate to White males, but the disparities clearly show that the glass and bamboo ceilings are alive—even in a company that is perceived to be "new". Women of color, in particular, are not visible at all levels of the organization (Stapleton, Gupta, Whittaker, O'Neil-Hart, Parker, Anderson, Gaber, 2018).

Although Google has increased its efforts to recruit women and non-White/non-Asian employees, they are more likely to be hired into non-technical positions. According to the Google Diversity Report (Google, 2018), in 2017 31 percent of the new hirees identified as female, 41 percent Asian, 3 percent black, 4 percent Latinx, and 45 percent White. However, for technical positions, the percentages of female, black, Latinx new hirees dropped: 25 percent identified as female, 2 percent black, and 3 percent Latinx. Asians were more likely to be hired into technical positions than any other race. Although Asians may be seen as the model minority in Alphabet and other hi-tech companies, the hiring along racial lines also reinforces the assumption that Asians in the US can only choose from a limited number of professions: technical positions are one of the few that are acceptable to mainstream society. When Asians are boxed into a few professions, it reinforces the perception that Asians are the same, and they lack individual characters. This perception has real-life consequences, as is reflected in the lawsuit against Harvard's race-based admissions practice, in which admissions officials characterized Asians as lacking individual characters (Gersen, 2018). Boxing in Asians also hinders their advancement into leadership position in all sectors, including an engineer-dominated company such as Alphabet.

An engineer-dominated culture that favors White males has real material consequences because it dictates who should be better rewarded. The salary disparity between engineers and non-engineers is staggering. According to a former employee,

> even if you ignore the extremes, such as top tier executives vs minimum wage contractors in certain roles, the difference in pay between highly ranked engineers and the non-engineers was remarkable. Factor of 10 pay difference for two people sitting near each other, albeit doing different jobs and with different skills, was not unheard of.
>
> (Nelson, 2016)

One Google, Two Worlds: The "Shadow" Workforce

The Non-Googlers

Job stratification across gender and racial lines only shows one picture of how inequitable the Alphabet workplace is. Under the same roof, temporary staff, vendors, and contractors (TVCs; hereafter contractors) work alongside the permanent workers, affectionately known as Googlers. Contractors are not only blue-collar workers at the cafeterias and security desks, they also find bugs in code, market new products, and moderate content (Glaser, 2018). The difference between Googlers and contractors begins with the hiring process: contractors are hired by staffing agencies, not Google, so they *do not make up the headcounts in Google's diversity report* (Glaser, 2018) even though more than half of the Google workforce is made up of contractors. In fact, these workers are *legally* not Google employees, they are not allowed to say they work *for* Google, but they work *at* Google (Dascalescu, 2017). Contractors exist as the negation, they are the *non*-Googlers. The negation status is not only characterized in employment terms, but also in work identity.

If contractors were counted as Alphabet employees, the workforce may be more diverse *but* also more inequitable. Race, gender, and geographical locations differentiate who are Googlers and who are contractors. The Tech Workers Coalition, a worker-led organization, suggested that contractors are disproportionately women and people of color. One former contractor wrote, "the minorities and women who make up much of the TVC workforce know that beggars can't be choosers. An imperfect job beats none when you need an income" (Livni, 2018, para. 15). One Googler mentioned that when she sees black women in Google, they are likely to clean up other people's mess or to guard the place (Glaser, 2018). Google also relies on cheap labor in India to handle tedious jobs such as labeling mapping data ("Inside Google's shadow workforce", 2018). Because contractors are not counted, the organizers of the Google walkout demanded that the company release "transparent data on the gender, race and ethnicity compensation gap, across both level and years of industry experience" (Stapleton et al., 2018).

However, it is also possible that contractors are more homogeneous because staff agencies rely on employees' referrals to recruit hirees. Because people tend to associate with others who are like them, personal referral may not be the best way to diversify the pool. Having said that, a former contractor suggested that Alphabet headquarters does not care all that much about the lack of diversity among contractors because they are not counted in the report any way (Weissman, 2013).

Employment status has material and cultural consequences for contractors; their workers' identities are composed of both the differences in employment terms and in work experiences. Like temporary workers in many industries, contractors do not enjoy Google healthcare, receive no retirement benefits, and have no long-term job security (Glaser, 2018). They are also denied the experience of the "real" Google culture: they are not invited to ski trips and town hall forums with the founders; they do not receive the same level of communication; and are barred from entering certain buildings on the work-site. The identity difference is marked by the color of the badge. Although they mix with Googlers, a careful look at the color of their badges will show that they are contractors. The denial to material benefits and cultural access uncomfortably echoes many gender, racial, and class exclusions in different societies over many historical time periods. It is particularly alarming when it takes place in a company that is branded as "new" and is deemed to be one of the best workplaces in the US.

The Invisibility of Non-Googlers Online and in the Workplace

A worker's identity is constituted online and in the workplace. In addition to the denial of a full Google experience, contractors are also rendered invisible online. Google's search engine, the company's prime product to search for information, is ironically a means to make contractors invisible to search engine users. When the keywords "Google jobs" are used, the links all show positions for permanent jobs. Users need to use "Google contractors" as keywords to search for information about the *non*-Googlers, which constitute more than half of the company's workforce. In contrast to the many websites devoted to how to get hired by Google, there are many fewer and shorter responses to the question of "what's it like to work at Google as a contractor?"[15] It is possible that current contractors are instructed to not talk about their work conditions, and it is also possible that they do not feel their self-representation is important. The invisible online status reinforces the assumption that contractors do not count.

At the workplace, contractors are also invisible. This sentiment was effectively summed up by the comment of a former contractor, "You're there, but you're not there" ("Inside Google's shadow workforce", 2018, para. 10). Some believe that contractors are treated as an underclass ("Inside Google's shadow workforce", 2018) and the distinction between Googlers and contractors constitutes a caste system (Livni, 2018). Others believe that contractors are almost like the servant class, they live and work around the house but are never seen by the masters ("Inside Google's shadow workforce", 2018).

Non-Googlers are believed to be less good than Googlers because only top-notch talents are believed to receive full-time contracts. The difference begins at the hiring stage. Googlers must only be hired in the proper way: the weeks-long interview process that tests technical skills and requires months of preparation. The *only* way to differentiate the cream of the crop from the rest is believed to be the screening tests that Google has created for itself. Even though Alphabet prides itself on being objective, the criteria were drafted by employees who already believed in the meritocracy ideology. If Alphabet uses nothing but objective criteria, then its own official website is sufficient. However, the multiple sites that advise people how to get hired by Alphabet show that aspiring workers should not only be excellent, but they should also be excellent *for Google*. How to be excellent for Google is subjective, therefore multiple websites are needed to describe what the culture is like. This begs the question whether being good enough for Alphabet is a culture fit or a set of objective technical skills. While the screening tests are supposed to be biasfree, some suggested that academic genealogy is very important to differentiate who will be hired in the proper way and who won't: "If you didn't go to Harvard, Stanford, Berkeley, MIT, or any of the top schools for business or [computer science], then contracting often *seems* like the only way into the wondrous world of Google while still being able to pay bills" (Anonymous, 2015a). The contractor's comment on paying bills should be noted because, as I suggested earlier, many sites that advise aspiring Googlers on how to get hired conveniently ignored the reality of financial needs. This comment pointed out that the screening process is not without bias, it privileges those who don't have immediate financial needs. For those who cannot afford to spend months studying for the tests and waiting to be hired, they can only begin as contractors.

The irony is that, even though contractors are deemed to be not as good as Googlers, they are deemed to be good *enough* to work with Googlers (Glaser, 2018). Contractors are thus imitators who "playact" Googlers. An anecdote shows that "playacting" will never allow contractors become real Googlers. A former contractor wrote that some temporary workers made themselves irreplaceable and filled in the slack left by Googlers when they were "doing yoga or going on trips" (Anonymous, 2015a). Yet their contracts were not renewed. To fill the void, Google hired *three new* contractors, rather than hiring the contractor as a permanent worker. This playacting is similar to the many instances in society when non-Whites, non-males playact the White men: they imitate the speech and the appearance, yet are still not invited to join the club.

Another instance to show how contractors "playact" Googlers is that the servants "playact" the masters when the masters are out of the house. According to a former contractor, on days when the full-time employees were at a retreat or at an all-hands meeting, the office would be staffed entirely by contractors. "We'd nibble on snacks from the office kitchen, contemplate whether to go to the pool or gym or yoga or dance classes, and laugh amongst ourselves at this heavenly employment hell" (Livni, 2018, para. 8).

Because contractors are not seen as *real* Googlers, they are not seen to do *real* jobs in a *real* workplace. One former contractor warned aspiring contractors that they needed to bear in mind that contractors are seen as outcasts, and it is "very tough for some to grasp when they thought they were accepting a *real* job" (Anonymous, 2015b, emphasis added). In addition, there is a perception that the *real* Google location is at the Alphabet headquarters in Mountain View—those who work in other US sites do not work at the *real* Google (Weissman, 2013).

Contractors' invisibility on the engine search and at the workplace hides their *real* economic contribution to the company. Because they are not *seen* as economically contributing to the company, they are mostly seen as peripheral to Alphabet's financial performance. In fact, Alphabet sees contractors as a potential liability. A leaked internal document revealed that the management treats contractors as potential hazards: "working with TVCs and Googlers is different. Our policies exist because TVC working arrangements carry significant risks" (as cited in Livni, 2018). This warning once again is similar to the many instances when non-Whites, non-males are seen as potentially dangerous or risky in some way in a well-functioning society. When non-Whites and non-males were invited to join mainstream society, they needed to be watched because they posed potential hazards to that society.

Why be a Contractor at Alphabet?

If contractors are treated as second-class citizens at Alphabet and if aspiring Googlers do have an agency to refuse subordination, why do so many smart people work as contractors? Some former contractors may harbor a victim mentality, but most still see the experience being positive. Some former workers suggested that young and innocent college graduates would easily fall into the trap of working as contractors because the Google brand is magical: "a young workforce is an uninformed workforce. [...] the promise of [Google's] name and the places it can take your career is just about enough to drown out the realities of working there" (Weissman, 2013). It is possible that temporary job recruiters prey on college graduates' mentality and pitch to them that a temporary job is a good way to get a foot in the door (Glaser, 2018).

However, most contractors firmly believe that, despite the second-class status, it is worthwhile to be exploited as contractors by Alphabet because of the meritocracy ideology. Contractors believe that as long as they work hard, they will become *real* Googlers; if not, they can still get a good job elsewhere. Even though some are highly aware of work inequities, they believe that personal merits will buck the system. On Quora, one former contractor said she and others "[had] lots of hope and support from my boss and my team for being converted (I was once told that I would get headcount if an engineer declined)" (Cheung, 2014). Another wrote:

> having Google on your resume will open doors and advance your career. I wouldn't have made as much progress in such a short period of time had I stayed on after my contract ended [...] work hard, earn respect, keep in touch with your Google colleagues, and look out for the right job.
>
> (Alecock, 2014)

The belief in meritocracy asks aspiring Googlers to assume personal responsibility for their own success and failure. However, individual merits do not explain why women and people of color are systematically not hired as Googlers. When both contractors and Googlers believe in the meritocracy ideology, there will not be any struggle between the two classes because they fail to see that the system has already categorized who are Googlers and who are not.

Another reason why contractors enjoy working at Alphabet is because of "perks", such as, for example, free food or an onsite gym. Somehow these perks are believed to compensate low salary, lack of job security, and the lack of tangible benefits such as healthcare or employer-contributed retirement accounts. For example, on Indeed.com,[16] Google contractors listed the pros of the workplace as free food and good colleagues. The cons were mostly structural problems such as poor pay and benefits, and short contracts. The emphasis on perks reinforces the "newness" of Alphabet. Because it is a new kind of company, so contractors believe that the company does not treat them like hourly service employees in other industries. By highlighting the perks and higher-than-average pay, Google contractors set themselves part from other hourly paid service workers such as retail sales associates and food industry workers. One former contractor rationalized that the differentiated treatment is not unfair because other companies are even worse (See, 2015).

The belief is that even though Alphabet contractors do not enjoy healthcare and other benefits, at least they have the privilege of free food and an onsite gym; even though contractors' pay is much lower than Googlers, at least they earn much more than other hourly paid workers in other industries. Once again, because non-Googlers work in a "new" company, they are still better off than contractors in "old" companies. The will to see themselves as second-class citizens in a "new" kind of company discourages contractors from establishing any sort of coalition with workers who are also in precarious positions in other industries.

Google as a Microcosm of the Economy?

One positive outcome of the employee walkout was that workplace problems were made visible and public. The mass of employees outside Google buildings showed the power of a collective, rather than a company of individuals. (It is, of course, with irony that contractors were discouraged to join the walkout). Responding to the disparate treatment of contractors and Googlers, Alphabet explained that contractors are necessary because the company does not have all the expertise, so they have to rely on specialists such as shuttle bus drivers and onsite doctors ("Inside Google shadow workforce", 2018). The spokesperson also explained that contractors are used to fill in unexpected job vacancies, such as maternity leave. However, both explanations are unsatisfactory because almost half the Google workforce are contractors. In addition, for a company that prides itself on data-driven decision-making, it is impossible for them to have such poor planning that they could not foresee if or when half the workforce would take unexpected leave. Moreover, for a company that is flush with cash, creating full-time positions for shuttle bus drivers and onsite doctors should not be a problem at all, especially when these employees are hired to promote "perks" that attract the best talent to the company.

The walkout organizers explained that the workplace problems at Alphabet are not restricted to Alphabet, but they reflect those in the "outside" world. The organizers suggested that the isolated and precarious feelings that Alphabet contractors have are felt by a lot of workers because "it's a *microcosm* of what's happening in the economy as a whole" ("Inside Google's shadow workforce", 2018, para. 7; emphasis added). The comment reflects the "exceptionalism" of Alphabet; even though it belongs to the global economy, somehow the company is "new" enough to be immune from the ills of the outside world. From an Actor-Network Theory perspective, Google is not a micro-site that reflects the macro-level economy, Google *is* the economy. In other words, Google has never been insulated from the "outside" world and "non-new" economies, its network *is* an economy. As shown in Chapter 4, "Political Profile", Google belongs to an actor-network of private ownership. While Google and other hi-tech companies, such as Amazon and Microsoft, are seen as powerful corporations, they are owned by investment banks and insurance companies, which in turn are owned by other banks and insurance companies. By being in the network, Alphabet needs to adopt the network characteristics: it needs to increase profits and reduce costs. No corporation that belongs to the network can escape from this fate. While some costs are seen as "fixed", such as hefty compensation for the most prized employees (i.e., the engineers), other costs are seen as flexible (such as contractors' salaries) ("Inside Google's shadow workforce", 2018).

Conclusion: Combating Culture with Culture

Alphabet is usually not seen as a culture manufacturer because it brands itself as a technology company. However, technology is not culturally neutral and value-free. I have argued that Alphabet has an engineer-dominated culture that fosters a meritocracy ideology. This ideology legitimizes gender, race, and class-biased hiring, promotion, and work equity. Current and aspiring employees believe that personal merits trump structural inequality. However, an examination of the workforce composition and employees' anecdotes show that non-White/non-Asian and non-male employees are less likely to be hired as engineers. Despite the fact that there are more Asian than White engineers, White males are more likely to be promoted to leadership positions. The recent walkout of Alphabet engineers raised awareness of workplace problems, ranging from sexual harassment to workplace inequities. However, inequities are seen as economic and policy issues, not as a cultural issue.

Ironically, culture is seen as a solution to combat economic disparities. The company and some employees use affect as a compensation to make up workplace inequities. To address job stratification between Googlers and contractors, a Google spokesperson said the company culture requires that everyone be treated with care and respect ("Inside Google's shadow workforce", 2018). A former contractor reinforced this by suggesting that he never felt discriminated against or excluded because "[the] company's culture seems to spawn an internal sense of *social equity* and *justice*" (See, 2015; emphasis added). In fact, this former contractor expressed his liking for being a contractor: "I *loved* being a contractor at Google" (See, 2015; emphasis added) because "Google was amazing".

By highlighting that an engineer-dominated company is not soulless but full of compassion, the Google spokesperson and the former contractor suggested that Alphabet does have a culture, and that this culture comes from the employees' own sense of justice and equity. Even if this perception is shared among the majority of employees, the belief in individual merits continues to reinforce the meritocracy ideology. The ideal Googlers are not only technically skilled but are also socially conscious. It further uplifts the company from being a technology company to being a humanitarian effort. By seeing Alphabet as a company that provides social goods for a more equal and just world, the company's expansion into non-search industries should only be applauded, not critiqued.

Notes

1 "The top 500 sites on the web". Alexa. www.alexa.com/topsites. Accessed: 13th December, 2018.
2 Alphabet. The world's most admired companies. *Fortune.* http://fortune.com/worlds-most-admired-companies/alphabet/ Accessed: 25th November, 2018.
3 Wildflower Schools. Our Network. https://wildflowerschools.org/our-network/ Accessed: 27th November, 2018.
4 Academics. Stanford University. www.stanford.edu/academics/ Accessed: 28th November, 2018.
5 Students. CalTech. www.caltech.edu/content/students. Accessed: 28th November, 2018.
6 Getting started: How to enroll. Foothill College. www.foothill.edu/reg/. Accessed: 28th November, 2018.
7 In-n-out Burger. Store Associate. www.in-n-out.com/employment/store-associate.aspx. Accessed: 20th November, 2018.
8 How it works. Google Careers. https://careers.google.com/how-we-hire/interview/#phone-hangout-interviews. Accessed: 20th November, 2018.
9 See endnote 8.
10 See endnote 8.
11 "How can I get a job at Facebook or Google in 6 months". Quora. www.quora.com/How-can-I-get-a-job-at-Facebook-or-Google-in-6-months-I-need-a-concise-work-plan-to-build-a-good-enough-skill-set-Should-I-join-some-other-start-up-or-build-my-own-projects-start-up-Should-I-just-focus-on-practicing-data-structures-and-algorithms. Accessed: 30th November, 2018.
12 Table 349. Degrees in computer and information sciences conferred by degree-granting institutions, by level of degree and sex of student: 1970–71 through 2010–11. Digest of Education Statistics. National Center for Education Statistics. https://nces.ed.gov/programs/digest/d12/tables/dt12_349.asp. Accessed: 21st January, 2019.
13 Google diversity. Our accelerated approach to diversity and inclusion. https://diversity.google/.
14 All topics. The United States Census Bureau. www.census.gov/quickfacts/fact/table/US/PST045217. Accessed: 5th December, 2018.
15 What's it like to work at Google as a contractor. Quora. www.quora.com/Whats-it-like-to-work-at-Google-as-a-contractor.
16 Google employee reviews for contractor. Indeed.com. www.indeed.com/cmp/Google/reviews?fjobtitle=Contractor. Accessed: 13th December, 2018.

Bibliography

Alecock, M. (2014, April 1). What's it like to work at Google as a contractor? *Quora*. Retrievedfrom: www.quora.com/Whats-it-like-to-work-at-Google-as-a-contractor. Accessed: 18th December, 2018.

Anonymous. (2015a, June 24). What are some notable differences between full-time employees and contractors at Google. *Quora*. Retrieved from: www.quora.com/W hat-are-some-notable-differences-between-full-time-employees-and-contractors-at-Google. Accessed: 16th December, 2018.

Anonymous. (2015b, August 5). What's it like to work at Google as a contractor. *Quora*. Retrieved from: www.quora.com/Whats-it-like-to-work-at-Google-as-a-contractor. Accessed: 3rd April, 2019.

Barthes, R. (1972). *Mythologies*. (A. Lavers trans.). New York: Hill and Wang. (Original work published 1957).

Benkler, Y. (2006). *The wealth of networks: How social production transforms markets and freedom*. New Haven, CT: Yale University Press.

Cheung, C. (2014, April 3). What's it like to work at Google as a contractor? *Quora*. Retrievedfrom: www.quora.com/Whats-it-like-to-work-at-Google-as-a-contractor. Accessed: 18th December, 2018.

Dascalescu, D. (2017, June 30). What's it like to work at Google as a contractor? *Quora*. Retrieved from: www.quora.com/Whats-it-like-to-work-at-Google-as-a -contractor. Accessed: 16th December, 2018.

Farias, I., & Mützel, S. (2015). Culture and actor network theory. In: N. J. Smelser & P. B. Baltes (Eds.), *International encyclopedia of the social and behavioral sciences* (2nd ed.) (Vol. 5, pp. 523–527). Amsterdam: Elsevier.

Foucault, M. (1971). *The order of things: An archeology of the human sciences*. New York: Pantheon.

Fuchs, C. (2013). Theorising and analysing digital labour: From global value chains to modes of production. *The Political Economy of Communication*, 2(1), 3–27.

Gassam, J. (2019). The best places to work in 2019. *Forbes*. Retrieved from: www. forbes.com/sites/janicegassam/2018/12/07/the-best-places-to-work-for-2019/#2 a056ffd528f. Accessed: 18th January, 2019.

Gersen, J. S. (2018, October 23). At trial, Harvard's Asian problem and a preference for white students from "sparse country". *The New Yorker*. Retrieved from: www. newyorker.com/news/our-columnists/at-trial-harvards-asian-problem-and-a-pref erence-for-white-students-from-sparse-country. Accessed: 18th January, 2019.

Glaser, A. (2018, December 5). Google's "Shadow workforce" has demands. *Slate*. https://slate.com/business/2018/12/google-walkout-protests-contract-workers .html. Accessed: 9th December, 2018.

Google. (2018). *Google diversity annual report 2018*. Mountain View, CA: Google. Retrieved from: https://static.googleusercontent.com/media/diversity.google/en// static/pdf/Google_Diversity_annual_report_2018.pdf. Accessed: 3rd April, 2019.

Google Walkout for Real Change. (2018, December 3). Invisible no longer: Google's shadow workfoce speaks up. *Medium*. Retrieved from: https://medium.com/@ GoogleWalkout/invisible-no-longer-googles-shadow-workforce-speaks-up-9 ea04b7bcc41. Accessed: 9th December, 2018.

Ingram, D. (2018, January 8). Ex-Google engineer fired over gender memo sues for discrimination. *Reuters*. Retrieved from: www.reuters.com/article/us-google-d iversity/ex-google-engineer-fired-over-gender-memo-sues-for-discrimination- idUSKBN1EX22L. Accessed: 20th January, 2019.

Inside Google's shadow workforce of contract laborers—many don't have health insurance. (2018). *Fortune*. Retrieved from: http://fortune.com/2018/07/25/google- contract-workers-contractor-jobs/. Accessed: 11th December, 2018.

Levy, S. (2011) *In the plex: How Google thinks, works, and shapes our lives*. New York: Simon & Schuster.

Livni, E. (2018, December 13). I was a contract worker in Google's caste system— and it wasn't pretty. *Quartz*. Retrieved from: https://qz.com/1494111/googles-cast e-system-is-bad-for-workers-and-bad-for-google-too/.

McRobbie, A. (2004). Post-feminism and popular culture. *Feminist Media Studies*, 4(3), 255–264.

Mosco, V. (2004) *The digital sublime: Myth, power, and cyberspace*. Cambridge, MA: MIT Press.

Nelson, J. (2016, July 24). What are some notable differences between full-time employees and contractors at Google. *Quora*. Retrieved from: www.quora.com/ What-are-some-notable-differences-between-full-time-employees-and-contractor s-at-Google. Accessed: 16th December, 2018.

Noonoo, S. (2018, November 20). Kid-tracking sensors may not be the wildest thing about this Montessori model. *EdSurge*. Retrieved from: www.edsurge.com/news /2018-11-20-kid-tracking-sensors-may-not-be-the-wildest-thing-about-this-mo ntessori-model. Accessed: 16th January, 2019.

Principles of management. (2010). *University of Minnesota Libraries Publishing*. Retrieved from: https://doi.org/10.24926/8668.1801.

Roth, L. M. (2006). *Selling women short: Gender, inequality on Wall Street*. Princeton, NJ: Princeton University Press.

See, B. (2015, December 4). What are some notable differences between full-time employees and contractors at Google. *Quora*. Retrieved from: www.quora.com/ What-are-some-notable-differences-between-full-time-employees-and-contractor s-at-Google. Accessed: 16th December, 2018.

Stapleton, C., Gupta, T., Whittaker, M., O'Neil-Hart, C., Parker, S., Anderson, E., & Gaber, A. (2018, November 1). We're the organizers of the Google walkout. Here are our demands. *New York Magazine*. Retrieved from: www.thecut.com/2018/11/ google-walkout-organizers-explain-demands.html?_ga=2.36322208.1437406877 .1544625240-1465147280.1544190409. Accessed: 16th December, 2018.

Wakabayashi, D., & Conger, K. (2018, October 26). Google workers fume over executives' payouts after sexual harassment claims. *The New York Times*. Retrieved from: www.nytimes.com/2018/10/26/technology/sexual-harassment-google.html. Accessed: 3rd April, 2019.

Weissman, R. (2013). A place at the foosball table: I was a Google contract worker. *GeekWire*. Retrieved from: www.geekwire.com/2013/place-foosball-table-google- contract-worker/. Accessed: 12th December, 2018.

6   Conclusion

At the beginning of the book, I set up a few challenges: first, I wanted to see Google as a process of *becoming*, not as *being*. As such, the founding of Alphabet is part of the becoming process rather than a transformative moment from one corporation to another. Second, I explored whether a political economy of communication is compatible with an Actor-Network Theory (ANT) approach. Third, I experimented with how computational methods of network analysis might be useful to a political economic critique of Alphabet. In addition, this book, as a volume collected in the *Global Media Giants* series, was also expected to illustrate how Alphabet accumulates power and wealth in capitalism. Just as capitalism is a contradictory political economic system, the examination of Alphabet as a *becoming* process also illustrates contradictions of how capitalism can be understood and critiqued. In the concluding chapter, I will first discuss whether the *Global Media Giants* chapter structure enables or constrains an analysis of networks. Then I discuss to what extent the analysis has shown the compatibility of a political economy of communication with ANT. Lastly, I evaluate the usefulness of computational methods to political economists.

Structures or Networks?

The *Global Media Giants* series invites authors to examine a major media/hi-tech corporation by examining its history and the three realms: economy, politics, and culture. Political economists highlight that capitalism has a history; they believe that the political-economic system that dominates most societies does not come from a vacuum, but as a result of struggles between classes, genders, races, and nation-states. Political economists also believe that the economy is not an autonomous realm of politics. Economic decisions are often made after political struggles. Although culture is usually not an area that political economists look at, culture legitimizes an unequal distribution of resources.

The separation of the three realms hinders an examination of Alphabet as a becoming process. From an ANT perspective, there is no macrostructure such as an economy, politics, and culture. Instead, ANT scholars prefer to examine how human and non-human actors assemble and dissemble themselves in a network. As such, no action is solely economic, political, or cultural (Farias & Mützel, 2015). In fact, ANT scholars reject the use of economic, political, or cultural reasons to explain actions (Latour, 2005; Law, 1999). The *Global Media Giants* book structure thus poses the first challenge of combining a political economy of communication and ANT. I drew on the concept of network, hoping to accommodate the different beliefs of whether a macrostructure exists or not. Instead of seeing the economy as a macrostructure, it is seen as a network of capital; instead of seeing politics as a macrostructure, it is seen as a network of power. For example, in Chapter 3, "Economic Profile", I suggested that the economic expansion of Alphabet depends on the infinite expansion of time. When users are invited to spend more time on Google products and when more users are invited to join the digital network, time appears to expand indefinitely. The expansion of time, however, is a question of economy as much as culture. Another example is the issue of labor. Even though labor is classified as a topic under the political realm by the editors, it is as much an economic issue and a cultural issue. In Chapter 5, "Cultural Profile", I explained the reason why Alphabet employees—most of them highly educated—tolerate work inequities and job segregation in the workplace is because of cultural beliefs. At a broader level, the Internet is about "newness"; inside the organization, a meritocratic, engineer-dominated culture is believed to solve all problems. Both cultural beliefs reinforce work inequities because Alphabet employees believe that "old" workplace problems do not occur in a "new" work culture.

The most important contradiction between macrostructure and network is illustrated by the notion of history. Political economists understand capitalism as a historical process; how resources are allocated among populations is a result of struggle. The history of Alphabet is then a history of the Internet, which is about the power struggle between the US military, the earliest computer enthusiasts, and commercial interests. However, in the writing of the history of Alphabet and the Internet, online information has become the source material. As Google Search organizes information in a specific way, the ontology of Alphabet's history needs to be critiqued, not accepted. This begs the question whether the understanding of the structure (i.e. a history of power struggles) can be independent of a network controlled by the power (i.e. online information provided by private corporations).

Despite the contradictions between macrostructure and network, both concepts are useful in an understanding of Alphabet as a corporation. Neither concept should be abandoned in future critiques of corporations in capitalism. In the following, I assess how ANT remedies three current shortcomings in a political economy of communication.

Can ANT Remedy Shortcomings in a Political Economy of Communication?

In the introductory chapter, I proposed that ANT and computational methods of network analysis could remedy three current shortcomings of a political economy of communication. First, political economists tend to see information as a monolithic commodity, that all information has the same quality. Second, political economists assume that humans are the only actors who have agency in social change. Third, political economists tend to avoid quantitative methods even though they see value in empirical data. Informed by the analysis, I evaluate in the following whether ANT has remedied these shortcomings, and what a future research direction might be.

I have pointed out in the introductory chapter that political economists tend to see information as having the same quality: either it is a public good or a commodity. There is little concern whether scientific knowledge that is publicly available has the same quality as phone numbers in a directory. Similarly, when information is seen as a commodity, the only difference between type of information is exchange value. However, an ANT perspective would argue that information is not passively waiting somewhere to be commodified, it has to be retrieved and organized by a search engine. Users also inform the search engines with what keywords to use to search and how to search. In turn, the search engine acts on the information and proposes to users what to do with that information. How information is understood, however, cannot be illustrated by merely examining documents. Interviews and ethnographic observation of human–information interaction are needed to understand the property and quality of information.

A second shortcoming of a political economy of communication is that it believes human beings are the only agents of change. This assumption ignores the powerful role that non-human actors (such as algorithms and digital devices) play in the information economy. I have already explained in the previous paragraph why algorithms actively shape how searches can be conducted. Another problem with ignoring non-human actors as change agents is that power is believed to reside with humans. This belief ignores the facts that humans have to make use of the material world in order to do things and that the material world in turn shapes how humans can act upon it and each other. To remedy the negligence of non-human agents in political economic research, ANT can draw attention to how human and non-human actors enable each other in a network: Actors on their own have no meaning, their meaning is given when they are in a network. With this in mind, a critique of power is a critique of how it is produced and distributed in a network. Chapter 4, "Political Profile", examined how power circulates in networks of corporate ownership, board of directors, and lobbying by examining the relations that connect individuals, organizations, and congressional bills together. Networks revealed some powerful yet often ignored actors in the Alphabet network: investment banks, insurance companies, professional organizations, and elite universities. The power of Alphabet has to be understood in relation to these often opaque relations.

The concept of network constituted by both human and non-human actors is, however, less effective at illustrating how power works through gender and race in an organization. In Chapter 5, "Cultural Profile", I examined how Alphabet's engineer-dominated culture uses meritocracy to justify who are legitimate Googlers and who are contract workers. The analysis mainly focused on gender, race, and class as macrostructures. I did not attempt to understand how non-human actors (such as machines, algorithms, and buildings) shape social identities in gender, race, and class because there was not an opportunity to observe how non-human actors shape human interactions. If there were opportunities to observe how humans interact with non-human actors, I may be able to understand how gender and race are constructed through discourses about machines and buildings.

The third shortcoming of a political economy of communication is its ambiguous stance toward empirical data. While political economists are skeptical of quantitative methods that isolate factors to explain communication processes, they generally believe in the epistemological and ontological values of empirical data such as financial data. Computational methods of network analysis are proven to be useful in a political economic critique of social relations. As shown in Chapter 3, "Economic Profile", and Chapter 4, "Political Profile", network analysis not only illustrates relations between actors, but it also shows the degree of the relations. Two useful visualizations are the networks shown in Figures 4.1 and 4.2 in Chapter 4. In Figure 4.1, I illustrated the power that shareholders have over hi-tech companies such as Alphabet, Microsoft, and Apple. Despite the assumed power of these hi-tech companies, their status of public companies reduced autonomous decision-making. At the same time, the ability to tap into the stock market means they can generate capital as long as they continue to be corporations with perceived high assets. Figure 4.2 shows relations between the board directors. The most powerful organizations are revealed to be professional organizations, elite universities, and venture capital firms. Computational methods, even at a descriptive level, strengthen a political economic critique of communication, because data visualization shows the strengths of social relations. It is also possible to expand the degrees of relations in a network, showing intriguing connections between individuals and organizations. Other networks that could be helpful in understanding an information economy are online connections (how having followers has become an economy) and imports/exports of Alphabet services (which services are available in which countries; or how local companies in different countries emulate Alphabet services). A computational method of semantic analysis will also reveal the sentiments expressed in the description of the company and the services: are they perceived positively or negatively? Semantic analysis will be helpful to understand the symbolic universe of a company to see if cultural values are assigned to products that are assumed to be value-free.

Bibliography

Farias, I., & Mützel, S. (2015). Culture and actor network theory. In: N. J. Smelser & P. B. Baltes (Eds.), *International encyclopedia of the social and behavioral sciences* (2nd ed.) (Vol. 5, pp. 523–527). Amsterdam: Elsevier.

Latour, B. (2005). *Reassembling the social: An introduction to actor-network theory*. Oxford, UK: Oxford University Press.

Law, J. (1999). After ANT: Complexity, naming and topology. In: J. Law & J. Hassard (Eds.), *Actor network theory and after* (pp. 1–14). Oxford, UK: Blackwell.

Index